Travel & Leisure Graphics

P·I·E BOOKS

Travel & Leisure Graphics

Printed in Hong Kong by Everbest Printing Co., Ltd.

P·I·E BOOKS
Villa Phoenix Suite 301, 4-14-6, Komagome, Toshima-ku,
Tokyo 170, Japan
Tel: 03-3949-5010 Fax: 03-3949-5650

ISBN 4-938586-87-8 C3070 P16000E

■

CONTENTS　目次

■

はじめに

■ 旅行業界は、近年にない不景気のなかで比較的好調であるといわれています。その理由として円高による料金の値下がり、休日数の増加などの他に、旅行の魅力そのものが時代にマッチしているという点もあげられるといえます。ゴージャスなホテル、風情あふれる温泉旅館、美しい景観の高原や、アクティブな南国リゾート... 旅の先にはいつも、日常生活とはかけはなれた夢の楽園が待っています。変化の激しい時代に生きる私たちの疲れを癒してくれるオアシス的存在として、ますます「旅行」人気が高まっているのではないでしょうか。本書に寄せられた作品を眺めながら、どこかほっとする気分になれた自らの体験からもその印象が強まりました。

「旅行」は古くから私たちの日常生活に浸透し愛されてきました。そんな普遍的な性質は広告にも反映されています。本書には都市部に限らず小さな町や村にいたるまで津々浦々から送られてきた作品が収録されています。グラフィックは都市から発信されるもの‥という常識を破り、バラエティー豊かな姿を見せています。また広く老若男女にアピールするためか、親しみやすい作品が多いのも大きな特長です。サービスという形のない商品をわかりやすく、魅力的に紹介しています。その際、特に凝った方法を選ぶよりは、写真、コピー、色という基本的な素材をいかに効果的に演出するかがこだわられています。全体的に多い情報量が、動きのあるレイアウト、メリハリあるコピー、カラフルな色づかい等の工夫で飽きずに、素早く読み取れるよう構成されているのです。旅行業界では日々、すさまじい勢いで様々な商品が提供されています。そのテーマを幅広いターゲットへ速やかにアプローチするために、シンプルながらも思わず目を捉えるような技が要求されるのだといえます。

今までグラフィックとしてまとめられる機会が少なかったこれらの作品を350点ものボリュームで編集した本書は、グラフィックのまた新しい一面を提示するチャンスとなると自負しています。旅行業界のみならず広告界全般の更なる発展をうながす資料としてお役立て頂ければ幸いです。最後に、この場を借りて制作に当たりご協力頂きました皆様に心よりお礼申し上げます。

ピエ・ブックス

FOREWORD

Despite the present economic recession - the most severe that Japan has encountered in recent memory - the travel industry continues to enjoy something of a boom. Besides the obvious reasons of ever-lower prices brought about by the soaring yen, and the longer holidays we are taking these days, there is also the important fact that the attractions of travel are well-matched to the times we live in. Glittering luxury hotels, hot-spring inns of style and character, resorts built in highlands overlooking magnificent vistas, or on tropical beaches offering sun, fun and water sports... the end of the journey promises a land of dreams, far removed from our usual mundane surroundings. Travel is also growing in popularity because it offers an oasis of relaxation, easing away the exhaustion that comes of modern life in our hectic, fast-paced world. Indeed, just glancing over the submissions featured in this book can induce that wonderful sense of gently unwinding...

Travel has long played an important role in our lives, and people certainly love the idea. Its universality is reflected in travel industry advertising. The artwork in this book originates from all sorts of nooks and crannies - small towns and even villages, as well as major cities. It belies the common wisdom that graphic design is an exclusive product of urban culture, and abounds in a rich variety of expression. Many samples are very easy to identify with, perhaps to appeal to the widest range of tastes - young and old, male and female. The 'products' featured, travel services, have no discernible shape, but are nevertheless put over in an attractive, easily understood way. Designers are not so concerned with fancy methods, but try to make effective use of the most basic tools: photos, written copy and colour. The total volume of information is cleverly presented to maintain interest with dynamic layouts, distinctive copy and bright colour, and it is all put together to give a clear portrayal of the message. The travel industry puts out all sorts of different products at dazzling speed. Simple, eye-catching techniques are needed to bring this information to the attention of a wide target audience.

This book is compiled from 350 examples of artwork in an area that up till now has seen little exposure of this sort, and we are proud to be opening up a further new avenue in graphic design. We hope this book will be a useful work of reference prompting interesting discoveries not only for the travel business but throughout the advertising world as a whole.

Finally, may we use this opportunity to express our deepest thanks to all those who assisted in the preparation of this book.

PIE Books

EDITORIAL NOTES

クレジット・フォーマット Credit Format

作品タイトル Title of work 使用目的 Intended use 制作年度 Year of completion A: Agency AD: Art director CD: Creative director CW: Copywriter D: Designer DF: Design firm E: Editor I: Illustrator P: Photographer PD: Producer

作品タイトルについてはクライアント名を表記し、その際、株式(有限)会社、財団法人、社団法人等の表記を省略しました。
Credits are headed by the name of the client. Full corporate titles have been abbreviated.

■   HOTELS, INNS AND RESORTS   ホテル・旅館・リゾート   ■

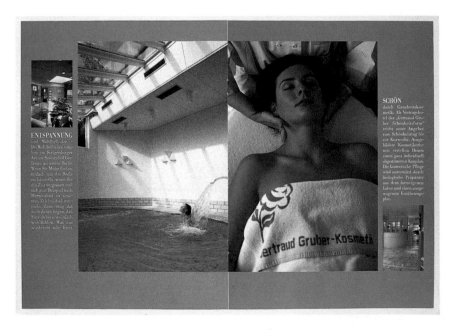

STEIGENBERGER AVANCE. VIER STERNE ZUM WOHLFÜHLEN.

BAD KREUZNACH heißt Sie herzlich willkommen. Ob Sie zur Kur kommen, die Ferien hier verbringen oder auf Tagungsreise sind - auf der Nahe-Insel in Bad Kreuznach genießen Sie Ruhe und Erholung. Denn Sie wohnen - eingefaßt von der Nahe - mitten im weitläufigen Kurpark, einem Flecken, fern der Hektik unserer Tage.

VIELES für die Fitness. Gleich vor dem Hotel beginnt der Kurpark. Und das ist ein geradezu ideales Terrain, um mit dem Fahrrad oder joggend den Kreislauf auf Trab zu bringen. Aber auch im Haus läßt sich sportlich aktiv sein: mit Kegeln und Schwimmen. Und nach dem persönlichen Fitnessprogramm schließt sich noch der eine oder andere Saunagang an.

WENIGER Stress, weniger Rauchen, den Körper entschlacken. In der Naturheilpraxis Pro Gesundheit arbeiten wir ein persönliches Programm für Sie aus. Sanfte Therapien, spezielle Massagen, Sauerstoff- und Aromabehandlungen geben neue Aktivität und steigern das körperliche Wohlfühlen.

BADEN gehen leicht gemacht. Das Thermal-Sole-Bad - die Crucenia Thermen - grenzt unmittelbar an das Hotel an und erwartet Sie mit konstanten 35° Celsius. Die Benutzung der Thermen ist für die Gäste unseres Hauses kostenlos.

SCHÖNHEIT muß bei uns nicht leiden, sie darf auf Erhalt, Ins Beauty-studio des Steigenberger Avance Kurhaus Bad Kreuznach geht die Haut in Kur. Und zwischt all die Strapazen und Belastungen ab, die Hektik und Stress mit sich bringen. Sie erhält die Pflege, die sie auf sanfte Weise wieder vital werden läßt. Ein Angebot übrigens, das für Damen wie Herren gleichermaßen gilt.

Steigenberger Hotels　ホテル/パンフレット　Hotel/Pamphlet　1992　P: Egon Binder

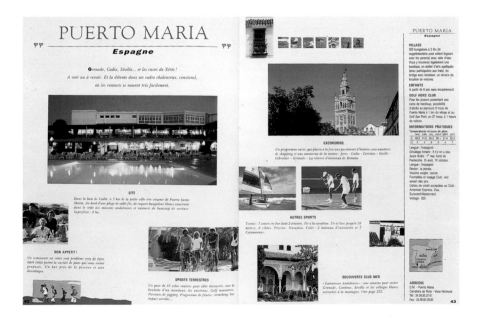

Club Mediterranée リゾート/パンフレット Resort/Pamphlet CD, AD, D: Alain Lachartre CD, CW: Philippe Blanchard P: Agencies & Club Mediterranée I: Jean-Philippe Delhomme DF: Vue Sur La Ville

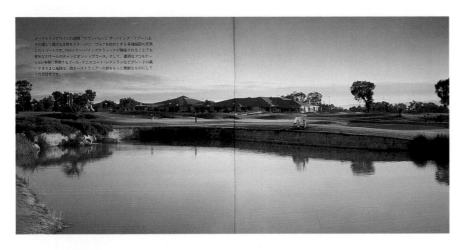

サンワ・バインズ Sanwa Vines　リゾート/パンフレット　Resort/Pamphlets　1989　CD, CW: 岡田元治 Ganji Okada　D: 新保健一郎 Kenichiro Shinpo　DF: ㈱ポパイ Popai, Inc.

東急ホテルチェーン Tokyu Hotel Chain　ホテル/オープン案内パンフレット　Hotel/Opening announcement pamphlet　1990　AD: 大橋清一 Seiichi Ohashi　D: 林 勝 Masaru Hayashi/相良多恵子 Taeko Sagara　P: 鶴田直樹 Naoki Tsuruta
CW: 杉谷一郎 Ichiro Sugitani　DF: ㈱CCレマン Les Mains Inc.

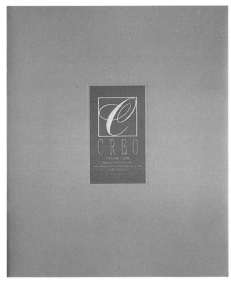

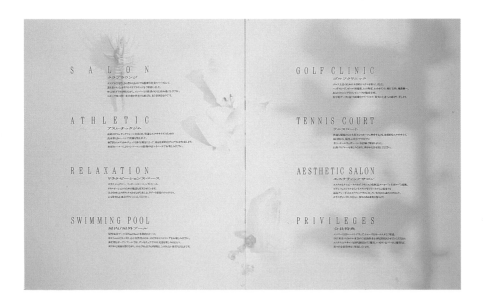

東急ホテルチェーン Tokyu Hotel Chain　ホテル/フィットネスクラブ・パンフレット　Hotel/Fitness club pamphlet　1990　AD: 大橋清一 Seiichi Ohashi　D: 林 勝 Masaru Hayashi/相良多恵子 Taeko Sagara　P: 鶴田直樹 Naoki Tsuruta
CW: 杉谷一郎 Ichiro Sugitani　DF: ㈱CCレマン Les Mains Inc.

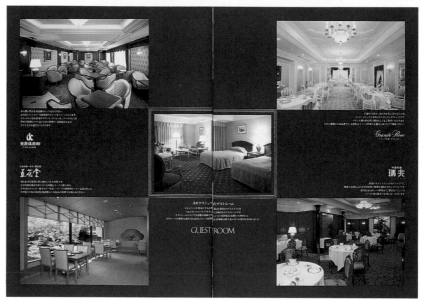

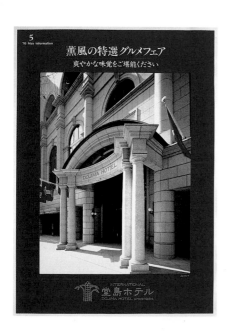

1. インターナショナル堂島ホテル International Dojima Hotel ホテル/フィットネスクラブ・パンフレット Hotel/Fitness club pamphlet 1994 CD: 東谷 裕 Hiroshi Higashitani P: 横山秀生 Shusei Yokoyama
 A: 伊藤忠ノマド㈱ Nomado Ltd.

2. インターナショナル堂島ホテル International Dojima Hotel ホテル/リーフレット Hotel/Leaflet 1995 CD: 森口誠久 Nobuhisa Moriguchi AD, D: 宮野康幸 Yasuyuki Miyano P: 光岡 豊 Yutaka Mitsuoka A: ㈱ディヴァイス Devise

1. インターナショナル堂島ホテル Intennrational Dojima Hotel　ホテル／ウェディング案内パンフレット　Hotel/Wedding services pamphlet　1994-95　CD: 東谷 裕 Hiroshi Higashitani　P: 横山秀生 Shusei Yokoyama
　　A: 伊藤忠ノマド㈱ Nomado Ltd.

2. インターナショナル堂島ホテル International Dojima Hotel　ホテル／ウェディング案内パンフレット　Hotel/Wedding services pamphlet　1995　CD: 東谷 裕 Hiroshi Higashitani　P: 義永庸人 Yasuhito Yoshinaga／光岡 豊 Yutaka Mitsuoka
　　A: 伊藤忠ノマド㈱ Nomado Ltd.／大新印刷 Daishin Printing Arts

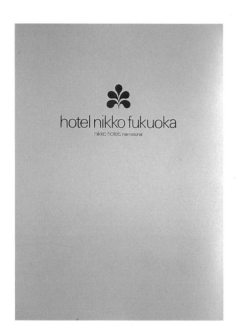

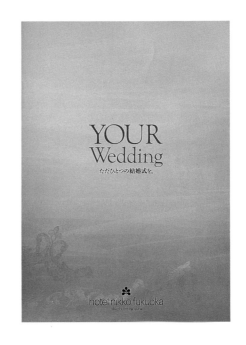

Photograph

Flower

Beauty up

YOUR
Wedding
ただひとつの結婚式を。

hotel nikko fukuoka

ホテル日航 福岡 Hotel Nikko Fukuoka ホテル/ウェディング案内パンフレット Hotel/Wedding services pamphlet 1995 CD: 宮下裕介（電通九州） Yusuke Miyashita
AD, DF: 高林秀明デザイン事務所 Takabayashi Shumei Design Corporation D: 垣田健一朗 Kenichiro Kakita P: 井上 一 Hajime Inoue CW: 佐藤栄子 Eiko Sato

新横浜グレースホテル New Yokohama Grace Hotel　ホテル/オープン案内ポスター　Hotel/Opening announcement posters　1990　AD, D: 天下井教子 Noriko Amagai　P: 島 隆志 Takashi Shima　CW: さとうみどり Midori Sato
DF: ㈲エーダッシュ A' Co., Ltd.

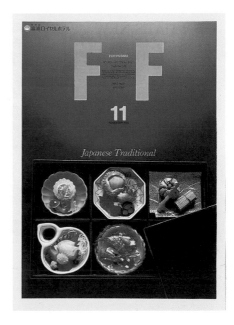

富浦ロイヤルホテル Tomiura Royal Hotel　ホテル/情報誌　Hotel/Newsletters　1992-93　CD, AD: 川名融郎 Michiro Kawana　D: 永井栄子 Eiko Nagai　P: 宮川幹夫 Mikio Miyagawa　CW: 家城大樹 Daiki Yashiro　DF: ㈱コア Core Corporation

エジュール、ホリデイプラザホテル Aijour In Pacific, Holiday Plaza Hotel　ホテル/パンフレット Hotel/Pamphlet 1993 CD, AD: 古山準一 Junichi Furuyama D: 中野 宏 Hiroshi Nakano P: 安福隆幸 Takayuki Yasufuku
CW: 竹下美香 Mika Takeshita DF: ㈱アルファード Alphad Co., Ltd.

The Hotel
STORIES

特集 = ホテル

歳月に磨きぬかれた古風なホテルから、すべては始まった。
じつに巧みにチップを受けとる老練のベルボーイにみちびかれ、
長期の滞在にふさわしい気のおけない部屋に案内される。
窓からの眺めを一眼に、手にとなげなパイプをゆらしながら、
ソファにもたれ、ここで過ごす日々に思いを馳せてみる。
橋の下を水心の水が流れていったものだ。
長い年月に訪れた、あの国・この街をめぐる記憶の旅が始まる……。

Text by 和泉 淳之 Junji Izumi

未知への好奇心がともづなを解き、
旅びとは、今日もまた夢想の土地をめざして出帆する。
ホテルとは、孤独な旅びとに安逸な眠りを約束する場所。
仮の宿にはあらず、人の生をあまねく集約した方舟。

ERASMUS
NHV HOTELS INTERNATIONAL MAGAZINE
1992 SUMMER Vol.1

SPECIAL FEATURE [THE HOTEL]

鏡の天蓋に映りこんだ一滴の光。
そこにゆらめく一縷を促えるために、
ホテルの朝は、あった。

NHVホテルズ インターナショナル、ハウステンボス NHV Hotels International, Huis Ten Bosch ホテル/情報誌 Hotel/Informtaion pamphlet 1992 CD: 岩坪敏和 Toshikazu Iwatsubo AD: 下村和代 Kazuyo Shimomura
P: 立木義浩 Yoshihiro Tatsuki

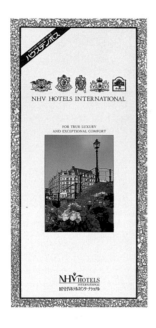

NHVホテルズ インターナショナル NHV Hotels International　ホテル/パンフレット Hotel/Pamphlets　CD: 岩坪敏和 Toshikazu Iwatsubo　AD: 下村和代 Kazuyo Shimomura　P: 立木義浩 Yoshihiro Tatsuki
DF: ㈱クリエイティブコア Creative Core

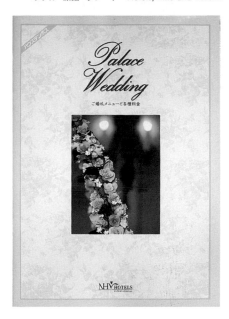

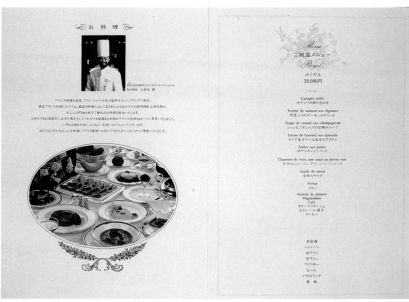

NHVホテルズ インターナショナル NHV Hotels International　ホテル/ウェディング案内パンフレット　Hotel/Wedding services pamphlets　CD: 岩坪敏和 Toshikazu Iwatsubo　AD: 下村和代 Kazuyo Shimomura
P: 立木義浩 Yoshihiro Tatsuki　DF: ㈱クリエイティブコア Creative Core

1. 東急電鉄、グランデコスキーリゾート Tokyu, Gran Deco ホテル＆スキーリゾート/ポスター Hotel & ski resort/Poster CD, AD: 遠山悦夫 Etsuo Toyama D: 楠井宙樹 Hiroki Kusui CW: 猪股 司 Tsukasa Inomata
 P (フォト合成): フォートン Foton

2, 3. 東急電鉄、グランデコスキーリゾート Tokyu, Gran Deco ホテル＆スキーリゾート/ポスター Hotel & ski resort/Posters CD, AD: 遠山悦夫 Etsuo Toyama D: 楠井宙樹 Hiroki Kusui P: 白鳥真太郎 Shintaro Shiratori
 CW: 猪股 司 Tsukasa Inomata Artwork: ビアード Beard

4. 東急電鉄、グランデコスキーリゾート Tokyu, Gran Deco ホテル＆スキーリゾート/ポスター Hotel & ski resort/Poster CD, AD: 遠山悦夫 Etsuo Toyama D: 楠井宙樹 Hiroki Kusui CW: 猪股 司 Tsukasa Inomata

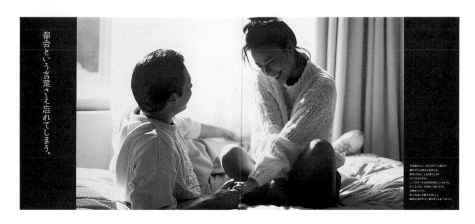

東急電鉄．グランデコスキーリゾート Tokyu, Gran Deco　ホテル＆スキーリゾート／パンフレット　Hotel & ski resort/Pamphlet　AD, CD: 遠山悦夫 Etsuo Toyama　D: 遠藤菊香 Kikuka Endo　CW: 猪股 司 Tsukasa Inomata

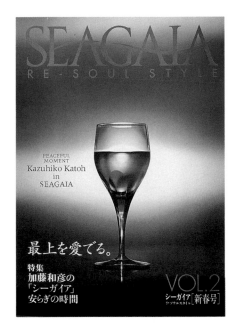

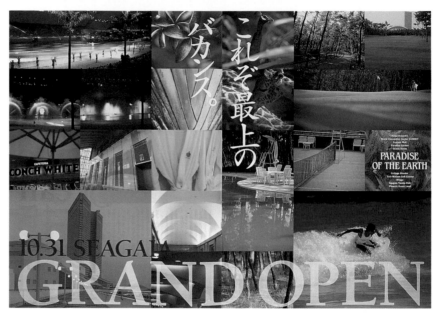

フェニックスリゾート, シーガイア Phoenix Resort, Seagaia　リゾート/パンフレット　Resort/Pamphlet　1993-94　DF: 大阪読売広告社 Osaka Yomiuri Kokoku Sha

1. 近鉄不動産、プライムリゾート賢島 Kintetsu Real Estate, Prime Resort Kashikojima　リゾート/会員募集DM Resort/Membership promotion DM 1994 CD: 仲 貢 Mitsuru Naka AD: 白瀧富士子 Fujiko Shirataki D: 赤石隆夫 Takao Akaishi
P: 亀岡清隆 Kiyotaka Kameoka CW: 筑城敏江 Toshie Tsuiki DF: ㈱ノバ Nova/㈱大広 Daiko Advertising Inc.

2. 近鉄不動産、プライムリゾート賢島 Kintetsu Real Estate, Prime Resort Kashikojima　リゾート/パンフレット Resort/Pamphlet 1993 CD: 仲 貢 Mitsuru Naka AD, D: 染井 勲 Isao Somei P: 亀岡清隆 Kiyotaka Kameoka
CW: 小野威夫 Takeo Ono DF: タッド大広 Tad Daiko A: ㈱大広 Daiko Advertising Inc. Planning: 水戸岡鋭治 Eiji Mitooka

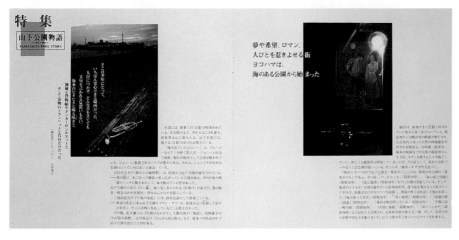

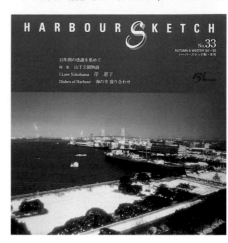

1. **ザ・ホテルヨコハマ** The Hotel Yokohama ホテル/情報誌 Hotel/Information pamphlet 1994 DF: ㈱ベイシス Basis

2. **ザ・ホテルヨコハマ** The Hotel Yokohama ホテル/パンフレット Hotel/Pamphlet 1995 A: 旭広告社 Asahi Kokokusha

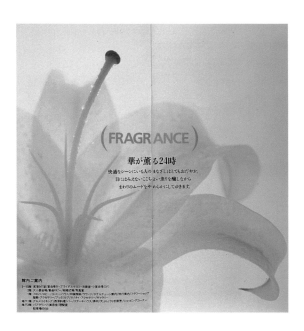

1. 新阪急ホテル Hotel New Hankyu　ホテル/パンフレット　Hotel/Pamphlet　1992　CD: 河内礼子 Reiko Kochi　AD: 宮下幸喜 Koki Miyashita　D: 田井里枝 Rie Tai　DF: ㈱アンクル Uncle Co., Ltd.

2. 新阪急ホテル Hotel New Hankyu　ホテル/情報誌　Hotel/Information pamphlets　1994-95　CD: 高石次典 Tsugumichi Takaishi　AD: 宮下幸喜 Koki Miyashita　D: 庄崎徹 Toru Shozaki　DF: ㈱アンクル Uncle Co., Ltd.

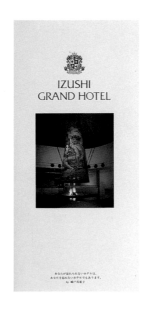

出石グランドホテル Izushi Grand Hotel　ホテル/パンフレット　Hotel/Pamphlets　D: 城戸真亜子 Maako Kido　DF: 吉田裕司事務所 Yoshida Yuji Office

LOCATION   ROOM

オアフ島南西部の海岸に広がるオーシャンフロントのコオリナ・リゾート内にあります。
ホノルル空港からは車で25分、白い砂浜と素朴な自然が残されたエリアにあります。
この「イヒラニ リゾート&スパ」はコオリナ・リゾート内の美しいラグーンに面しています。ここから眺める夕陽は、いつまでも心に残るような美しさです。

客室は、62㎡以上の広々としたつくりで、ほとんどの部屋からは海かラグーンを見渡すことができます。ゆったりとしたラナイ（バルコニー）はクイーンメリー・スタイルのラウンジ・チェアが置かれ、海を眺めながらお食事も楽しめます。居心地の良さを大切に考えたインテリアは、グリーンで落ち着いたイメージにコーディネイト、大理石が敷きつめられたバスルーム、ガラス張りのシャワールームなど、洗練された贅沢感をあじわえます。大型ディスプレイのカラーテレビ、ミニバー、そして天井には南の島の雰囲気たっぷりのファンなど、どれをとってもご満足のいただけるものです。

パーティーは会話から始まる…

スリリングな美しさに少しだけ胸が高鳴る。
友人と二人で招かれたパーティーは、危険な香りが漂っていた。
思い思いに着飾った人達はキラキラと輝き、その怪しい光に魅せられて、引き込まれていく自分がいた。
ゲームを楽しむかのように始まった会話。初めてはめた白い手袋が、しぐさや言葉をおしゃれにしてしまう。
「明日の夕方、会えない？」
2:00pm いつもだったらYESなのに、今日の私は、なぜかYES

DINING   SPA

「Azul」全米トップ10に選ばれたシェフによるクロスカルチャーキュイジーヌを豊富な世界のワインセレクションと共に、超一流のディナータイムをどうぞ。
「Naupaka Terrace」オープンエアーのテラスから海を眺めながらのコンチネンタル料理など。
日本料理レストラン「医庵」、ハワイ屈指の本格的な懐石料理から、お手軽な和食までご用意しております。また、毎日カウンターもございます。

イヒラニ・スパは3,352㎡の屋内屋外施設をもつハワイ初の本格的スパです。オランダセラピーといわれる海水や海藻を用いた海洋療法をはじめ、スウェーデン式マッサージ、ハーブラップ、アロマテラピーなど各種のアイテムにより、究極のリラクゼーションが得られます。また、スパレストランでのヘルシーメニュー、スパプールやフィットネスセンターでの様々なエクササイズ、ボディ、フェイス、ヘアーなどトータルなビューティ・プログラム、さらには、セラーやサロンでのメンタル・ケアなど、本格的なスパプログラムが用意され、最高の環境で心身ともにリフレッシュすることができます。

少しだけ、心が動いた…

コバルトに輝く水しぶきを眺めながら、ハイビスカスを添えたドリンクに手を伸ばす。
ふと視線を感じる。ふと顔を上げると、3つ先のテーブルに、1人の少年の姿があった。
あの純粋な瞳は何を考えているのだろう…
日の濃い場に居る私。
あんなに真っすぐ人をみつめることができるのは、心がきれいな証拠かもしれない。
少年に笑みを返してみる。あわてるその少年の瞳、慌ててストローを口にしたら、グラスにはもう水しか残っていないのに…
5:00pm 少年のまなざしに、少しだけ、心が動いた。

1. **日本航空、イヒラニ リゾート** Japan Airlines, Ihilani Resort & Spa ホテル/パンフレット Hotel/Pamphlet 1994 AD: 清水正行 Masayuki Shimizu D: 遠藤恵子 Keiko Endo CW: 坪倉優司 Yuji Tsubokura
   DF: ㈱アルファルファ Alfalfa Design Studio
2. **草津ナウリゾートホテル Kusatsu Now Resort Hotel** ホテル/パンフレット Hotel/Pamphlet 1994 CD: 青木伸年 Nobutoshi Aoki, AD, D: 佐藤美里 Misato Sato P: 久保田昌義 Masayoshi Kubota CW: 萱場由起 Yuki Kayaba
   DF: ㈱エイエイピー AAP Co., Ltd.

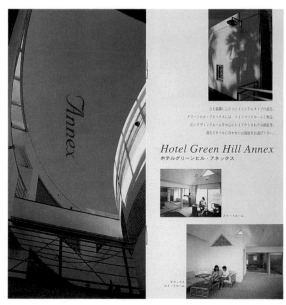

1. カターラ福島屋 Katara Fukushimaya　ホテル/パンフレット　Hotel/Pamphlet　CD: 青木伸年 Nobutoshi Aoki　AD, D: 時田勇都 Hayato Tokita　P: 山本和英 Kazuhide Yamamoto　CW: 黒木孝宏 Takahiro Kuroki　DF: ㈱エイエイピー AAP Inc.

2. ホテルグリーンヒル白浜 Hotel Green Hill Shirahama　ホテル/パンフレット　Hotel/Pamphlet　1995　CD, AD: 岩高清美 Kiyomi Iwataka　D: 前田 剛 Takeshi Maeda　P: 垂井俊憲 Toshinori Tarui　DF: ㈱室永デザイン Muronaga Design

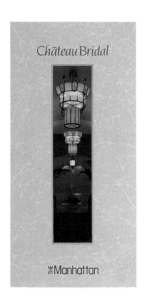

1. ホテル ラ シエネガ Hotel & Restaurant La Cienega　ホテル/パンフレット　Hotel/Pamphlet　1993　AD: 子田幸一 Koichi Koda　D: 小池礼子 Reiko Koike　P: 長沢廣司 Koji Nagasawa　I: 大久保ハジメ Hajime Okubo
　CW: 黒木孝宏 Takahiro Kuroki　DF: エイエイピー 小田原支店 AAP Odawara Br.　Planning: 杉山裕秋 Hiroaki Sugiyama

2. ザ・マンハッタン The Manhattan　ホテル/ウェディング案内パンフレット　Hotel/Wedding services pamphlet

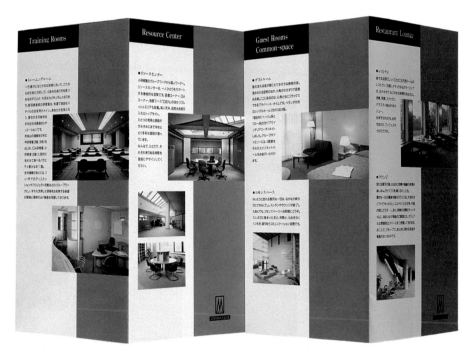

1. 九州キヨスク、ホテルブラッサム福岡 Kyushu Kiosk, Hotel Blossom Fukuoka　ホテル/パンフレット Hotel/Pamphlet 1992 DF: ㈲高林秀明デザイン事務所 Takabayashi Shumei Design Corporation

2. プラス、音羽倶楽部 Plus, Otowa Club　宿泊施設/リーフレット Rest house/Leaflet 1993-94 D: 富田ルツ Rutsu Tomita/小島美代子 Miyoko Kojima DF: ㈲イクスース・アゴラ Ikusu:su Agora Co., Ltd.

3. 紀州鉄道、那須塩原ホテル Kishu Tetsudo, Nasu Shiobara Hotel　ホテル/パンフレット Hotel/Pamphlet CD: 相沢義忠 Yoshitada Aizawa AD: 片山 学 Manabu Katayama D: 前田太志 Futoshi Maeda CW: 豊田 浩 Hiroshi Toyoda
Editorial Director: 宮崎 晃 Akira Miyazaki

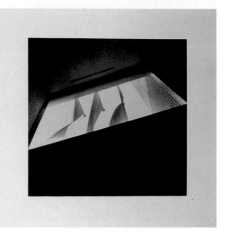

ロテル・ド・ロテル L'Hotel De L'Hotel ホテル/パンフレット Hotel/Pamphlet 1990-94 CD, AD, D: ㈱ビギ Bigi Co., Ltd. P: 山下恒徳 Tsunenori Yamashita

那須野ケ原ベルビューホテル Nasunogahara Belview Hotel　ホテル/パンフレット　Hotel/Pamphlet 1993 CD, AD, I: 境 修一郎 Shuichiro Sakai　D: 前原由紀夫 Yukio Maehara　P: 田代泰三 Taizo Tashiro　CW: 山形公一 Koichi Yamagata DF: ㈱ボーダー Border Inc.

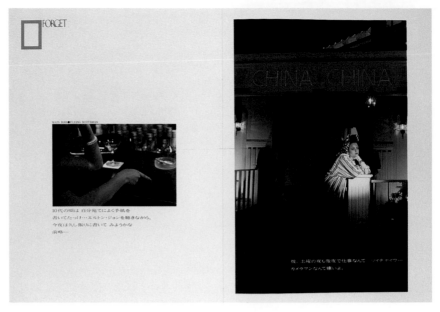

HOTEL BOOK
A TOTALLY NEW CONCEPT IN HOTEL PLANNING

HIGHLAND RESORT

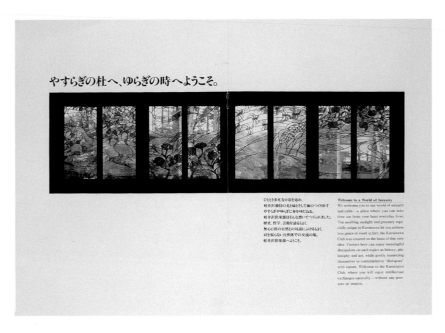

やすらぎの杜へ、ゆらぎの時へようこそ。

ひとときまばゆい日常を忘れ、
軽井沢倶楽部の光と緑とそして風のつくり出す
やすらぎやゆらぎに身をゆだねる。
軽井沢倶楽部はそんな想いでつくられました。
歴史、哲学、芸術を語るほどに
無心に枕との自然との対話におけるほど、
肩を張らない自然体での交流の場。
軽井沢倶楽部へようこそ。

Welcome in a World of Serenity
We welcome you to our world of serenity and calm—a place where you can take time out from your busy everyday lives. The soothing sunlight and greenery especially unique to Karuizawa let you achieve true peace of mind: in fact, the Karuizawa Club was created on the basis of this very idea. Visitors here can enjoy meaningful discussions on such topics as history, philosophy and art, while gently immersing themselves in contemplative "dialogues" with nature. Welcome to the Karuizawa Club, where you will enjoy intellectual exchanges naturally—without any pressure or tension.

満ちているのは知のスパイラル。

自然体の知的交流。
人の心を開放し、心の豊かさをやすらぎのなかでの
対話を可能にする心地良い空間。
そこで自分に、そっとに、そして知のうちにリラックスして
語り、論じ、想い、楽しむ。
知のスパイラル実感は、明日への新しいハーモニーは、
こうして生まれる。
タンマ時を楽め過ごしているいでしょうか。

Bustling with Intellectual Activity
We provide a place where intellectual exchanges flow naturally. The Karuizawa Club's highly stimulating atmosphere enables a wide range of discussions amidst a relaxing and tranquil setting that "opens" people up. Here is an intellectually charged environment where all can converse, debate, contemplate and enjoy in an earnest, enthusiastic and, above all, relaxing manner. And such an environment can lead to the creation of a new harmonious balance for tomorrow—Are you feeling a little tense these days?

軽井沢倶楽部
KARUIZAWA CLUB

富士ゼロックス株式会社

秘めているのは、多彩な文化の香り。

軽井沢の歴史と、先人たちの足跡の中に
つけ込まれた文化と知性の香り。
そうした知のたずまいにはうんとんで
しかも親しい思地を感じさせる。
訪問する客をまず迎える門扉の鳥。
ユーモラスに笑いかける石灯篭。
そして人のふれあいの誘いを今象徴するあみ・あみ・き、
設計者の想いが、い沢い渡るときにこめられています。

Deep Inside—the Allure of a Colorful Culture
Our forefathers of Karuizawa left behind a legacy of great cultural and intellectual merits, both of which have merged into the overall appearance of this famous resort area. At the same time, there is an air of newness about the place. Designers of the Karuizawa Club have expressed their ideas through the creation of some truly charming works: the bird figures on the club's entrance gate that seem to greet arriving visitors; the stone lanterns with humorous smiles; and the front entrance's parasol-patterned ceiling, under which people can gather for friendly encounters.

富士ゼロックス、軽井沢クラブ Fuji Xerox, Karuizawa Club 宿泊施設/パンフレット　Rest house/Pamphlet　1993　CD, CW: 伊知地義雄 Yoshio Ijichi　D: 小林正直 Masanao Kobayashi　P: 小原健志 Takeshi Ohara

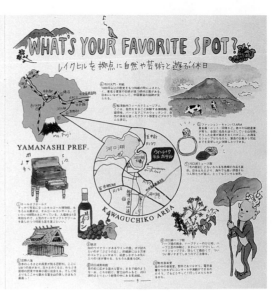

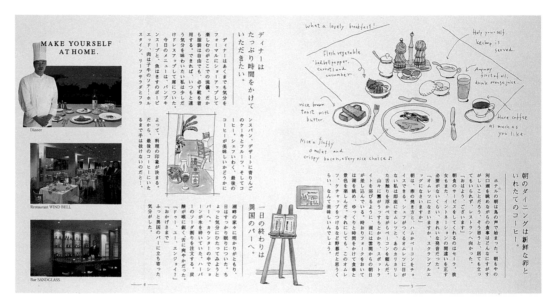

1. ウインレイクヒルホテル Win Lakehill Hotel　ホテル/パンフレット　Hotel/Pamphlet　CD: 川島英司 Eiji Kawashima　AD, D: 本多 集 Tsudou Honda　P: 青柳 茂 Shigeru Aoyagi　I: 平野恵理子 Eriko Hirano　CW: 山下敬子 Keiko Yamashita

2. 斑尾高原開発 Madarao Heights Development　ホテル/パンフレット　Hotel/Pamphlet　1991　CD, CW: 船生みわ Miwa Funyu　AD, D: 長 信一 Shinichi Cho

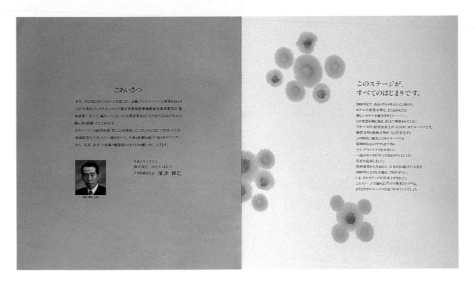

1. ホテルハマツ Hotel Hamatsu　ホテル/オープン案内パンフレット　Hotel/Opening announcement pamphlet 1991 CD: 本橋一郎 Ichiro Motohashi AD, D: 朝長康典 Yasunori Tomonaga P: 酒井あさじ Asaji Sakai
I: 増永広春 Koshun Masunaga CW: 経塚 清 Kiyoshi Kyozuka DF: ㈲パワーミックス Power Mix Co., Ltd.

2. 富士屋ホテル Fujiya Hotel　ホテル/季刊情報誌　Hotel/Quarterly magazines 1994-95

その日のわたしに。

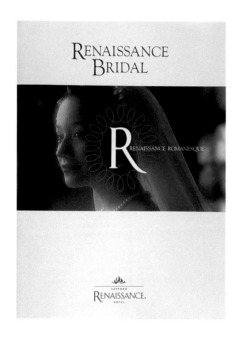

RENAISSANCE
BRIDAL

RENAISSANCE ROMANESQUE

SAPPORO
RENAISSANCE
HOTEL

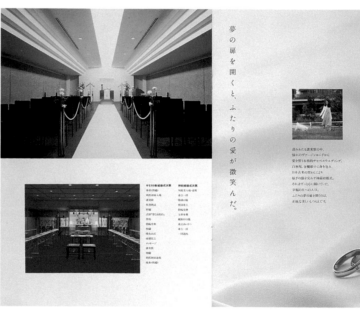

夢の扉を開くと、ふたりの愛が微笑んだ。

喜びの想いを飾る、幸福というメニューがある。

サッポロ ルネッサンス ホテル Sapporo Runaissance Hotel　ホテル/ウェディング案内パンフレット　Hotel/Wedding services pamphlet　1994　AD: 藤井義貴 Yoshitaka Fujii　D: 山田雅裕 Masahiro Yamada　P: 戸木 誠 Makoto Toki
DF: ㈲アイテック Itec Inc.　A: ㈱ピーアールセンター PR Center Co., Ltd.

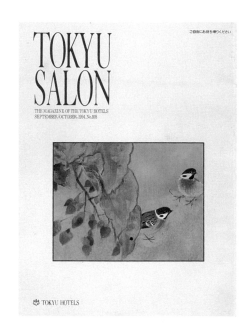

1. 姫路キャッスルホテル Himeji Castle Hotel　ホテル/パンフレット　Hotel/Pamphlet　1992　AD: 首藤成利 Shigetoshi Shuto　D: 井口幸恵 Yukie Iguchi　P: 藤森久嘉 Hisayoshi Fujimori　I: 山根峯章 Mineaki Yamane　DF: ㈱ビーエス PS Co., Ltd.

2. 東急ホテルチェーン Tokyu Hotel Chain　ホテル/情報誌　Hotel/Information pamphlet　CD, CW: 小林好雄 Yoshio Kobayashi　D: 竹下博文 Hirofumi Takeshita/印南ゆう子 Yuko Innami/相沢直樹 Masaki Aizawa/日高倫子 Michiko Hidaka/
松尾玲子 Reiko Matsuo　P: 柴崎潤二 Junji Shibazaki

3. 秋田キャッスルホテル Akita Castle Hotel　ホテル/ウエディング案内パンフレット　Hotel/Wedding services pamphlet　1993　AD, D: 戎谷 等 Hitoshi Ebisuya

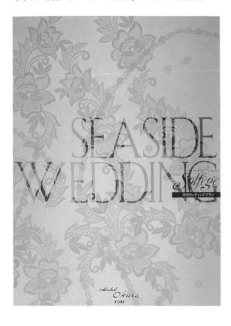

1. ホテル オークラ神戸 Hotel Okura Kobe　ホテル/ウェディング案内パンフレット　Hotel/Wedding services pamphlet　1989　CD, AD: 古山準一 Junichi Furuyama　D: 中野 宏 Hiroshi Nakano　P: 稲生義弘 Yoshihiro Inao /
安福隆幸 Takayuki Yasufuku　CW: 竹下美香 Mika Takeshita　DF: (株)アルファード Alphad Co., Ltd.

2. ホテル オークラ神戸 Hotel Okura Kobe　ホテル/情報誌　Hotel/Information pamphlets　1994-95　CD: 古山準一 Junichi Furuyama　AD, D: 中野 宏 Hiroshi Nakano　P: 稲生義弘 Yoshihiro Inao/安福隆幸 Takayuki Yasufuku
CW: 竹下美香 Mika Takeshita　DF: (株)アルファード Alphad Co., Ltd.

ゆったりと満ち足りて

やすらぎにつつまれて

美食の旅、心ゆくまで

ここは、都市のオアシス

1. ホテルセンチュリーハイアット Hotel Century Hyatt Tokyo　ホテル/パンフレット　Hotel/Pamphlet　P: 加藤正博 Masahiro Kato　DF: ㈱コミュニケーション・メントース Communication Mentors Co., Ltd.

2. ホテルセンチュリーハイアット Hotel Century Hyatt Tokyo　ホテル/パンフレット　Hotel/Pamphlet　P: ジャスティン チャン Justin Chan　DF: ㈱コミュニケーション・メントース Communication Mentors Co., Ltd.

フォーシーズンズホテル 椿山荘 Four Seasons Hotel Tokyo at Chinzan-so ホテル/パンフレット Hotel/Pamphlets 1991-94

1. ホテルニューオータニ幕張 Hotel New Otani Makuhari　ホテル/ウェディング案内パンフレット　Hotel/Wedding services pamphlet　CD, AD, D: 志賀孝道　Takamichi Shiga　I: 石倉ヒロユキ　Hiroyuki Ishikura
　 CW: 本間善朗　Yoshiaki Honma

2. ホテルニューオータニ幕張 Hotel New Otani Makuhari　ホテル/ウェディング案内パンフレット　Hotel/Wedding services pamphlet　CD, AD, D: 志賀孝道　Takamichi Shiga　P: 大西治良　Haruyoshi Onishi　CW: 本間善朗　Yoshiaki Honma

3. ホテルニューオータニ幕張 Hotel New Otani Makuhari　ホテル/ウェディング案内パンフレット　Hotel/Wedding services pamphlet　CD, AD, D: 志賀孝道　Takamichi Shiga　P: 安達洋次郎　Yojiro Adachi

世界で培ったホスピタリティが息づいています。
ホテル日航金沢

Gracious hospitality awaits you at the Hotel Nikko Kanazawa

A comfortable chair placed conveniently in the lobby; an attractive painting casually adorning the wall of your room; the warm smile of welcome at the door; the extra care and courteous service that make the time you spend in the hotel so pleasant - these are only a part of the gracious hospitality that awaits your stay at the Hotel Nikko Kanazawa.
Nikko Hotels International's worldwide experience, gracious service and spacious accommodations make the Hotel Nikko Kanazawa as pleasant a place to stay as any of the famous hotels of Europe and America. The international resort atmosphere, together with the careful attention that we pay to the small details, helps to induce the mental and physical relaxation so desired by the busy globetrotting business executive. Advanced facilities, stylish interiors, superior service, gourmet menus, and most important of all, a courteous and skilled staff ready to care for your every need - all designed for the convenience of traveling executives.

インペリアルスイート　Imperial Suite

リビングルーム　Living Room

ベッドルーム　Bedroom

バスルーム　Bathroom

hotel nikko kanazawa

ホテルは、大人の時間を包んでいます。
The Hotel - A Time and Place for You

Community Town

JAL Ticketing Counter
あなたの長旅を爽やかにサポート。

In "Porte Kanazawa," next to the Hotel Nikko Kanazawa, the JAL Ticketing Counter on the first floor can help you make flight reservations and give you all sorts of information to make your stay more enjoyable. Drop in at the counter, and we can recommend many interesting nearby spots.

Fitness Club
エグゼクティブを憩いの場所。

On the 4th and 5th floors of "Porte Kanazawa," the Central Fitness Club Kanazawa is entrusted as being first class. The Hotel Nikko Kanazawa has an affiliation with the Central Fitness Club Kanazawa so that hotel guests may make use of the facilities - swimming pool, gym, exercise machines, sauna bath, jacuzzi. Refresh yourself while staying in our hotel.

Fashion Gallery
ファッションの街、ポルテ金沢。

On offer are a variety of fashion boutiques on the 1st, 2nd and 3rd floors. Come and enjoy shopping or just browsing. The elegant display windows catch your eye with their magnificent clothes, jewelry, fashion goods and lots more.

Art Hall
美しい調べを奏でるアートホール。

On the 6th floor of "Porte Kanazawa" is the multi-purpose "Kanazawa Citizen's Art Hall" with 304 comfortable seats for the enjoyment of musical concerts, plays, dramas, lectures, and the like. Constructed to the latest in spacious acoustic designs and equipped with the newest audio technology, this brand new hall is drawing attention as Kanazawa's first new art spot.

ホテル日航金沢 Hotel Nikko Kanazawa ホテル/パンフレット Hotel/Pamphlet 1994 CD, AD: 五寳利男 Toshio Goho D: 東 康弘 Yasuhiro Azuma P: 品野与四寛 Yoshihiro Shinano/吉尾正洋 Masahiro Yoshio CW: 大波加光男 Mitsuo Ohaka DF: ㈱バルデザイングループ VAL Design Group Co., Ltd.

1. **Disney Development** ホテル/パンフレット　Hotel/Pamphlets　1988　CD: David Carter　AD, D: Sanio Lai　DF: David Carter Design
2. **Rosewood Hotels** ホテル/パンフレット　Hotel/Pamphlets　1988　CD: David Carter　AD, D: Laura Graham　DF: David Carter Design

1. **Disney Development** ホテル/パンフレット Hotel/Pamphlets 1990 CD: Lori B. Wilson AD, D: Randall Hill P: FPG International Stock/Trisha Wilson DF: David Carter Design

2. **Grand Hyatt Bali** ホテル/パンフレット Hotel/Pamphlets 1991 CD: David Carter AD, D: Lori B. Wilson I: Jacenda Lai DF: David Carter Design

ラディアント ホテル Radiant Hotel　ホテル/パンフレット、ポスター　Hotel/Pamphlet, Posters　DF: ㈱キーンズ Keens Company

6:25 A.M. At the break of day

エントランスの"柱"は
〈コロシアム・イン・蓼科〉の表徴。
ホテルを支えるこだわりと
主張が見えます。

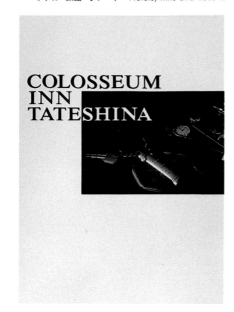

COLOSSEUM INN TATESHINA

7:35 A.M. Refresh morning in the sunshine

モーニングコールは小鳥達のさえずり。

THE CROSSING HALL（クロッシングホール）

HOTEL

RISTORANTE

遊びごころを刺激する
エンターテインメントホテル イル パラッツォ。

HOTEL
IL PALAZZO

INFORMATION

1. コロシアム イン 蓼科 Colosseum inn Tateshina　ホテル/パンフレット　Hotel/Pamphlet
2. ホテル イル パラッツォ Hotel Il Palazzo　ホテル/パンフレット　Hotel/Pamphlet

伊東ホテル聚楽 Ito Hotel Juraku　ホテル／パンフレット　Hotel/Pamphlets　CD, AD, D: 吉岡幸郎 Yukio Yoshioka　P: 青木年伸 Toshinobu Aoki　CW: 黒木孝宏 Takahiro Kuroki

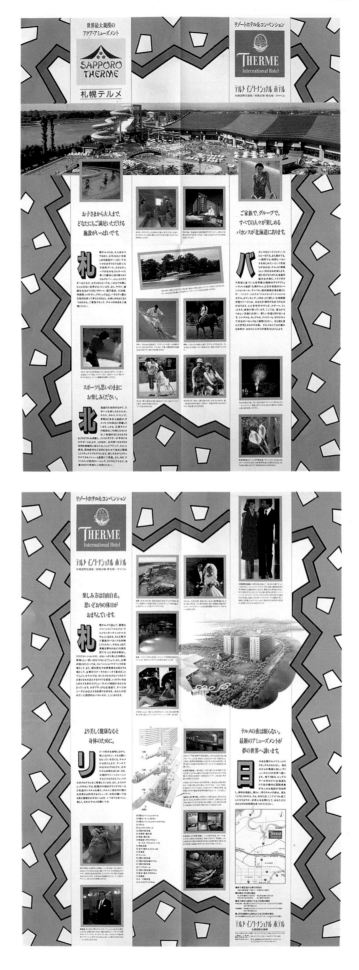

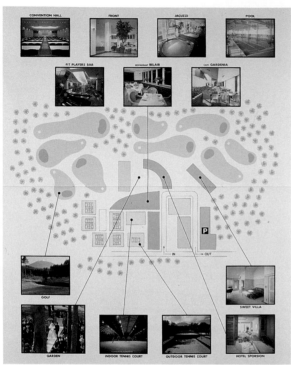

由布の大地に、人と自然の新しいドラマが芽生えて。

ロマンは、実現してロマンである。

馬の背中って、意外に高くて心地よい気分です。

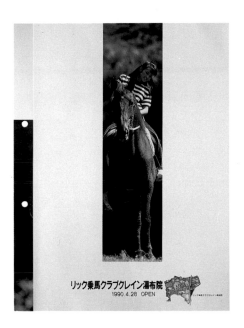

リック乗馬クラブクレイン湯布院
1990.4.28 OPEN

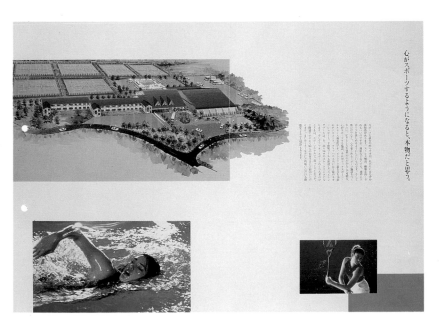

心がスポーツするようになると、本物だと思う。

リックスポーツルネサンス湯布院
1990.7 OPEN

リック スプリング ヴァレー RIC Spring Valley　リゾート／パンフレット　Resort/Pamphlet　1990　CD: 塩本久子 Hisako Shiomoto　AD, D: 泉 明 Akira Izumi　P: 福本正明 Masaaki Fukumoto　CW: 馬場善樹 Yoshiki Baba

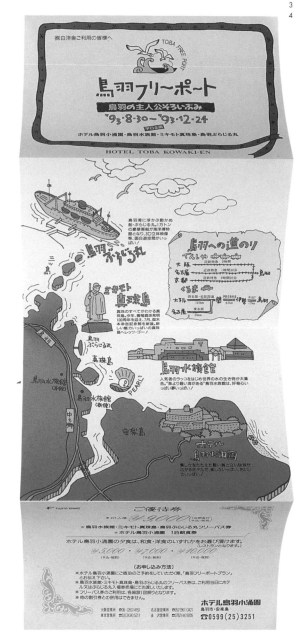

1. 鳥羽小涌園 Hotel Toba Kowakien　旅館/チケット　Japanese inn/Tickets　CD: 池田憲一 Kenichi Ikeda　AD, D: 三部不二子 Fujiko Sanbe

2. 鳥羽小涌園 Hotel Toba Kowakien　旅館/案内状　Announcement　1993　CD: 池田憲一 Kenichi Ikeda　AD, D: 三部不二子 Fujiko Sanbe　I: ㈱ジップス 前川尚子 Naoko Maekawa

3. 鳥羽小涌園 Hotel Toba Kowakien　旅館/パターゴルフ場案内、チケット　Japanese inn/Mini golf information, tickets　1994　CD: 池田憲一 Kenichi Ikeda　AD, D: 三部不二子 Fujiko Sanbe

4. ホテル鳥羽小涌園 Hotel Toba Kowakien　旅館/パンフレット　Japanese inn/Pamphlet

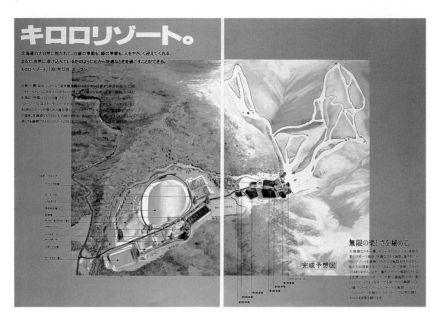

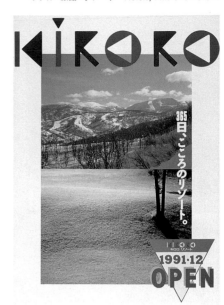

キロロリゾート Kiroro Resort　リゾート/パンフレット　Resort/Pamphlets 1991 CD, CW: 七野清豪 Seigo Shichino AD: 本間稔朗 Toshiro Honma D: 本間夏子 Natsuko Honma I: 佐藤英幸 Hideyuki Sato/福士千香子 Chikako Fukushi
DF: ㈲絵文 EMON

Nikko Prestige Resort

CHUZENJI KANAYA HOTEL

Nikko National Park
Prestigious Resort

Prestigious Resort

日本におけるフライフィッシングアクラブ発祥の地であり、鱒釣りのメッカである中禅寺湖や、国絵植物の宝庫といわれる湿々な自然と、見院室に代表される多くの文化財。加えて首都圏から近い立地条件は、リゾートとしても最高のステージです。
私たちが目指すのは Prestigious Resort

Four Seasons in Nikko

Spring *Summer*

ヤシオツツジやヤチケラの山桜花が春の訪れを告げます。シャクナゲの群落、山桜といっせいに咲いて山の春をかたたえます。

シラカバ、ミズナラの新緑が初夏を知らせます。ニッコウキスゲやワタスゲの花が咲き春釣の色や虫の緑も活気に満ちあふれる季節です。

Luxurious Rooms

Luxurious Rooms

客室からミズナラの日本ごしに湖紙を望めます。
ベランダに出て湖と湖の特気を深呼吸、心もからだもリフレッシュ──。
お部屋は6つのタイプをご用意いたしております。

Kanaya Hotels in Nikko

Kanaya Hotels in Nikko

日光金谷ホテルの創業は1873年（明治6年）6月。明治の香りを残した現存する日本最古のホテルとしてご愛顧をいただいております。
「お客様を第一に、真心をこめたお返し」をモットーとし中禅寺金谷ホテルとともに、愛されるホテルを目指しております。

Other Facilities

中禅寺金谷ホテル Chuzenji Kanaya Hotel　ホテル/パンフレット　Hotel/Pamphlet　1991　D, P, I, CW: 渡辺 稔 Minoru Watanabe　DF: ㈱シーダー Cedar Co., Ltd.

札幌での117年を資産として、
サッポロビールは新たな飛躍の時を迎えました。

サッポロビールの歴史は、1876年、日本人による最初の本格的なビール工場「開拓使麦酒醸造所」に始まります。それ以来、「ビールへのまじめ」という愛着で札幌市民の皆様に見守られ、サッポロビールは、世界的な企業へと成長しました。いま、その117年の歳月を最大の資産として、サッポロビールは新たな地歩の時を迎えています。

そして、1989年、長く親しんでいただいた札幌第一製造所が惜別の時を迎え、何物にも替え難い、札幌市民の皆様からいただいた温かな気持ちに感謝して、その跡地に皆様のための新しい文化の発信地となる「生活工房・サッポロファクトリー」を誕生させました。屋内公園、レストラン、ミュージアム、コンサートホール、企業パビリオンなどなど、札幌の歴史を刻んだ赤レンガ建築を保存しながら、飲食、スポーツ、ビジネス、教育など、さまざまな生活文化を発信していく、これは、新しい街です。そのコンセプト、一機能として生まれたのがホテルクラビーサッポロ。札幌に暮らす人々、札幌を訪れる人々の生活をより豊かにできればと願っています。

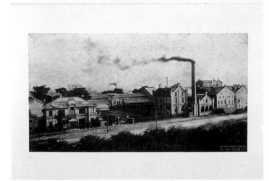

メンバーのようにゲストをもてなす。
新しい快適への発想です。

ホテルクラビー・サッポロ。その「クラビーCLUBBY」とは、気持ちのいい、人付き合いのいい、という意味を持ちます。初めて訪れたゲストにも、メンバーのように自由で居心地のいい時間を過ごしていただく、訪れる機会を重ねるごとに快適さが深まっていく。そして、ゲストとホテルの、あるいはゲスト同士の、親しく打ち解ける交流が生まれて、いちだんとクラブウェルに似た気分と機能を備えているホテル、それがホテルクラビー・サッポロです。

そのために大切にしたのは、過剰なサービスではなく、実質的なサービスの充実にこだわること、古き良き時代に、ホテルが持っていたホスピタリティスタイルこそ、私たちの目指すおもてなしです。調度であり、高質で品位です。さらに、従来のメジャーなホテルづくりとは一線を画し、デザインやアートなどの各分野から一流の発想や感性、美意識を結集。ゲストのひとつひとつにつながるアートワークのように仕立てておりました。一方で「生活工房・サッポロファクトリー」内のアイマックス

シアター、フィットネスクラブ、天然温泉を使用した都市型クアミューズメント・スプリングスなど、最新のサービスへの優待利用といった特典にも留意するなど、私たちのホテルクラビー・サッポロは、ホテルの新しい快適を、皆様に提供しています。

ロビーに訪れたその時から、
上質なクラビー・ライフは約束されます。

ホテルクラビー・サッポロは、ロビーを三つのバーンに分けています。私たちにとって、ロビーはただ単にゲストをお迎えし、お見送りするだけの場所ではありません。まず正面入り口に続く〈セントラルロビー〉、いたくつに広らのみを求めるのでなく、快適さと機能性を追求し、コンシェルジュ・デスクも備えました。お打ち合わせや和やかな歓談・お見送りも、ちょっとした歓談にご利用いただけます。フロントデスクのある〈もてもてプションロビー〉、チェックイン、

チェックアウトをはじめ、さまざまなサービスの窓口として、ゲストとホテルの接点がここで行われ、そして〈ゲストロビー〉。ライティングデスクを用意し、読書を楽しんだり、ワープロ、パソコンを使用してのビジネスワークをこなしたり、サッポロビール博物館所蔵の古書をあしらい〈ライブラリー〉としても機能します。歓談するゲストたちのさまざまな目的に、高いクオリティで応えると三つのロビーに、クラビーならではの個性が、ここにも現れています。

「パストデザイン」がイメージしたのは、ホスピタリティやサービスに高い完成度を見せた"30年代のホテル"。その洗練されたホテルリビングのスタイルを再現しました。メープル〈楓〉の肌合い・白が調和した室内は、上品な佇まい。調度は、黒茶とクロームパイプの組み合わせにした、落ち着きがあり、品格があり、それでいて、明るくやわらかさがある。クラビーの名に恥じない、快適な滞在のための空間です。

欽山 Kinzan　旅館/施設案内パンフレット　Japanese inn/Facilities pamphlets　1994　CD: 宮垣真二 Shinji Miyagaki　AD: 半田泰明 Yasuaki Handa　D: 長戸俊道 Toshimichi Nagato　I: 中道 淳 Jun Nakamichi　CW: 増田隆一 Ryuichi Masuda
DF: ㈱モノリス Monolith, Inc.

南楽 Nanraku　旅館/パンフレット　Japanese inn/Pamphlet　CD: 山本房史 Fusashi Yamamoto　AD, D: 時田勇都 Hayato Tokita　P: 山本和英 Kazuhide Yamamoto　CW: 黒木孝宏 Takahiro Kuroki　DF: ㈱エイエイピー AAP Inc.

茶寮 宗園 Saryo Soen 旅館/パンフレット　Japanese inn/Pamphlet　1994　CD, CW: 菅井孝明 Takaaki Sugai　AD, D: 星澤初美 Hatsumi Hoshizawa　P: プロフィックス・河野スタジオ Prophix・Kano Studio

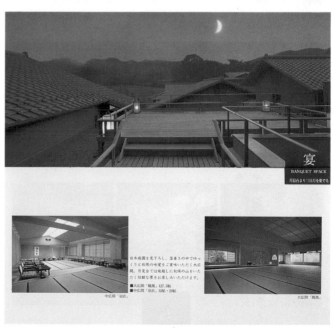

茶寮 宗園 Saryo Soen 旅館/パンフレット Japanese inn/Pamphlets 1994 CD, CW: 菅井孝明 Takaaki Sugai AD, D: 星澤初美 Hatsumi Hoshizawa P: プロフィックス・河野スタジオ Prophix・Kano Studio

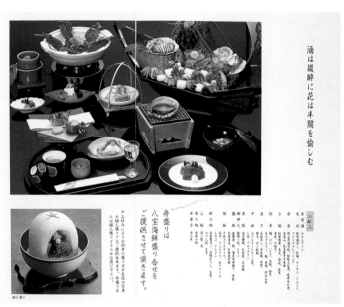

稲取 銀水荘 Inatori Ginsuiso 旅館/パンフレット Japanese inn/Pamphlets DF: ㈱エイエイピー AAP Inc.

稲取 銀水荘 Inatori Ginsuiso 旅館/パンフレット　Japanese inn/Pamphlet　DF: ㈱エイエイピー AAP Inc.

ホテル河鹿荘 Hotel Kajikaso　旅館/パンフレット　Japanese inn/Pamphlet　1992　AD, D: 垣野健一 Kenichi Kakino　P: 山本和英 Kazuhide Yamamoto　CW: 島野敬之 Takayuki Shimano　DF: エイエイピー小田原支店 AAP Odawara Br.
Planning: 須田紀哉 Toshiya Suda

著莪の里 ゆめや Shoganosato Yumeya 旅館／パンフレット　Japanese inn/Pamphlet 1992 CD, CW: 内村 愛 Chikashi Uchimura AD, D: 佐藤美里 Misato Sato P: 木村浩之 Hiroyuki Kimura
DF: ㈱エイエイビー新潟支店 Ad Art Planning, Co., Ltd. Niigata Br.

藤田観光.緑酔苑 Fujita Kanko, Ryokusuien 旅館/パンフレット　Japanese inn/Pamphlet　1991-92　CD: 吉岡幸郎 Yukio Yoshioka　AD, D: 時田勇都 Hayato Tokita　P: 青木伸年 Nobutoshi Aoki/伊藤 剛 Tsuyoshi Ito　I: 鈴木 誠 Makoto Suzuki
CW: 鈴木冬野 Fuyuno Suzuki　DF: エイエイピー小田原支店 AAP Odawara Br.　Planning: 雲野悦武 Yukitake Unno

藤田観光、緑酔苑 Fujita Kanko, Ryokusuien 旅館/パンフレット　Japanese inn/Pamphlet　1993　CD: 木内正浩 Masahiro Kiuchi　AD: 吉岡幸郎 Yukio Yoshioka　D: 時田勇都 Hayato Tokita　P: 伊藤 剛 Tsuyoshi Ito　CW: 黒木孝宏 Takahiro Kuroki
DF: エイエイピー小田原支店 AAP Odawara Br.　Planning: 渡辺朝也 Tomoya Watanabe

1. **本陣枠月 Honjin Suigetsu** 旅館/パンフレット Japanese inn/Pamphlet 1994 CD: 斉藤竹彦 Takehiko Saito AD, D: 五十嵐昭好 Akiyoshi Igarashi CW: 木本宅治 Takuji Kimoto

2. **本陣粋月 Honjin Seigetsu** 旅館/パンフレット Japanese inn/Pamphlet 1994 CD: 斉藤竹彦 Takehiko Saito AD, D: 五十嵐昭好 Akiyoshi Igarashi CW: 二村志保 Shiho Futamura

兵衛向陽閣 Hyoe Koyokaku 旅館／パンフレット Japanese inn/Pamphlets 1994 CD: 藤原一宏 Kazuhiro Fujiwara AD, D: 山口由香子 Yukako Yamaguchi

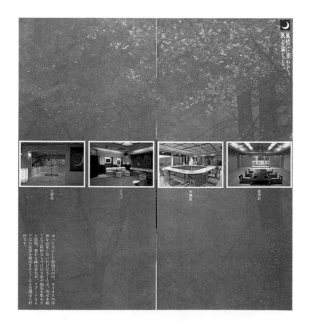

1. 奈良屋 **Naraya** 旅館/パンフレット　Japanese inn/Pamphlet　1994　CD, AD, D: 宇都宮理人 Masato Utsunomiya　P: 小南善彦 Yoshihiko Kominami　CW: 伊藤正貴 Masaki Ito

2. 和心亭豊月 **Washintei Hogetsu** 旅館/パンフレット　Japanese inn/Pamphlet　1993　CD, CW: 木内正浩 Masahiro Kiuchi　AD, D: 渡辺晴美 Harumi Watanabe　P: 小南善彦 Yoshihiko Kominami/長沢廣司 Koji Nagasawa
DF: エイエイピー小田原支店 AAP Odawara Br.　Planning: 杉山裕秋 Hiroaki Sugiyama

1: 湯元館 Yumotokan　旅館/総合案内パンフレット　Japanese inn/General information pamphlet　CD: 名倉昌志 Masashi Nakura　AD, D, I: 三部不二子 Fujiko Sanbe　P: 小南喜彦 Yoshihiko Kominami　CW: 二村志保 Shiho Futamura

2: 玉屋旅館 Tamaya Ryokan　旅館/パンフレット　Japanese inn/Pamphlet　1994　CD, CW: 阿倍正行 Masayuki Abe　AD, D: 神村 潔 Kiyoshi Kamimura　P: 宮田泰明 Yasuaki Miyata

ホテル楊貴館 Hotel Yokikan　旅館/パンフレット　Japanese inn/Pamphlet　1994　AD, D: 神川ちなみ Chinami Kamikawa

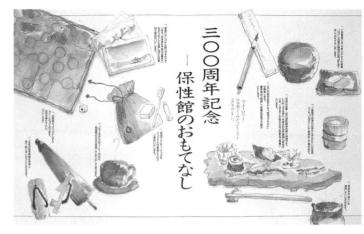

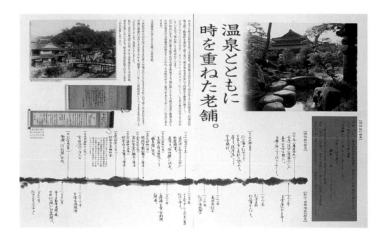

保性館 Hoseikan　旅館/300周年記念案内　Japanese inn/300th anniversary celebrations announcements　1994　CD: 藤原一宏 Kazuhiro Fujiwara　D, I: 神川ちなみ Chinami Kamikawa

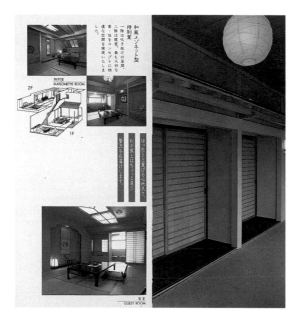

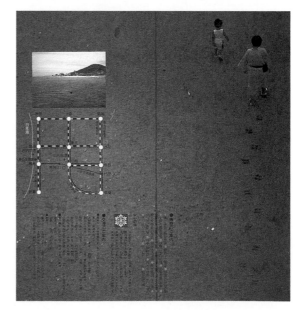

いさごや Isagoya 旅館/パンフレット　Japanese inn/Pamphlet　1990　AD: 星澤初美 Hatsumi Hoshizawa　D: ファワード Foward　P: ニュープレス New Press　CW: 松尾公輝 Koki Matsuo

三朝館 Misasakan 旅館/パンフレット Japanese inn/Pamphlet 1994 CD: 斉藤竹彦 Takehiko Saito AD, D: 山口由香子 Yukako Yamaguchi P: 中野充三 Juzo Nakano

1. たちばな四季亭 **Tachibana Shikitei** 旅館／ダイレクトメール　Japanese inn/Direct mail　1995　CD: 谷内聖仁 Kiyohito Taniuchi　AD, D, I: 三部不二子 Fujiko Sanbe

2. たちばな四季亭 **Tachibana Shikitei** 旅館／礼状　Japanese inn/Appreciation card　1995　CD: 谷内聖仁 Kiyohito Taniuchi　AD, D, I: 三部不二子 Fujiko Sanbe

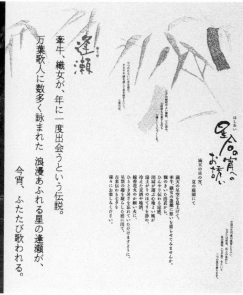

逢瀬

牽牛、織女が、年に一度出会うという、浪漫あふれる星の逢瀬が、

今宵、ふたたび歌われる。

今宵 月のあかりに招かれて

杯に浮かぶ淡い光とたわむれる。

ほのかにして、風情あり。

凛として海に咲く

冬の花を味わいましょう。

ゆらり揺れるあかりのもとで

畳の上にくつろいで。

1. 清流荘 Seiryuso　旅館/パンフレット　Japanese inn/Pamphlet　CD: 青木伸年 Nobutoshi Aoki　D: 時田勇都 Hayato Tokita　P: 山本和英 Kazuhide Yamamoto

2. 岩の湯 Iwanoyu　旅館/パンフレット　Japanese inn/Pamphlet　1994　AD, D: 佐藤美里 Misato Sato　I: 房州久美子 Kumiko Bosyu　CW: 三原清一 Seiichi Mihara　DF: ㈱エイエイピー AAP Co., Ltd.

1
2

1. **伍楼閣 Gorokaku**　旅館/パンフレット　Japanese inn/Pamphlet　1994　CD, AD, D: 佐藤美里 Misato Sato　P: 宮田泰明 Yasuaki Miyata　CW: 阿部正行 Masayuki Abe　DF: ㈱エイエイピー AAP Co., Ltd.

2. **対岳楼 林屋 Taigakuro Hayashiya**　旅館/パンフレット　Japanese inn/Paamphlet　1994　CD, CW: 伊藤正貴 Masaki Ito　AD, D: 宇都宮理人 Masato Utsunomiya　P: 小南善彦 Yoshihiko Kominami

1. 阿しか里 Ashikari　旅館/パンフレット　Japanese inn/Pamphlet　1990　DF: ムク・プランニング Muku Planning

2. 西浦グランドホテル Nishiura Grand Hotel　旅館/パンフレット　Japanese inn/Pamphlet　DF: オオゼキ写真印刷㈱ Ozeki Shashin Insatsu

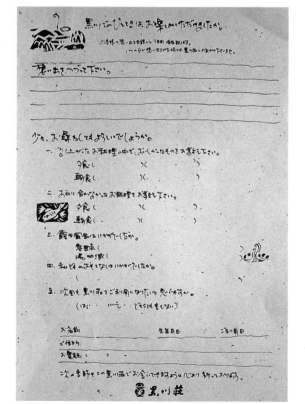

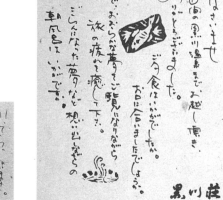

1. 黒川荘 Kurokawa-So 旅館/パンフレット Japanese inn/Pamphlet

2, 3. 黒川荘 Kurokawa-So 旅館/メッセージ・カード Japanese inn/Greeting cards 1995 CD: 高木義勝 Yoshikatsu Takagi AD, D, I: 三部不二子 Fujiko Sanbe

4. 黒川荘 Kurokawa-So 旅館/アンケート Japanese inn/Questionnaire 1995 CD: 高木義勝 Yoshikatsu Takagi AD, D, I: 三部不二子 Fujiko Sanbe

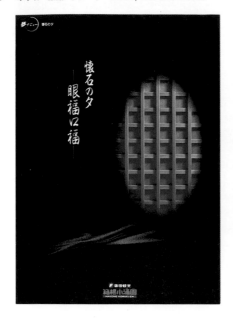

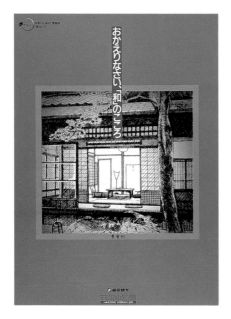

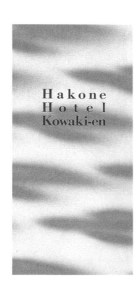

1. 藤田観光、箱根小涌園 Fujita Kanko, Hakone Kowakien　旅館／リーフレット　Japanese inn/Leaflet　1991-92　CD: 吉岡幸郎 Yukio Yoshioka　AD, D: 時田勇都 Hayato Tokita　P: 青木伸年 Nobutoshi Aoki／伊藤 剛 Tsuyoshi Ito
I: 鈴木 誠 Makoto Suzuki　CW: 鈴木冬野 Fuyuno Suzuki　DF: エイエイビー小田原支店 AAP Odawara Br.　Planning: 雲野悦武 Yoshitake Unno

2. 藤田観光、箱根小涌園 Fujita Kanko, Hakone Kowakien　旅館／リーフレット　Japanese inn/Leaflet　1991-92　CD: 吉岡幸郎 Yukio Yoshioka　AD, D: 時田勇都 Hayato Tokita　P: 青木伸年 Nobutoshi Aoki／伊藤 剛 Tsuyoshi Ito
I: 鈴木 誠 Makoto Suzuki　CW: 鈴木冬野 Fuyuno Suzuki　DF: エイエイビー小田原支店 AAP Odawara Br.　Planning: 雲野悦武 Yoshitake Unno

3. 藤田観光、箱根ホテル 小涌園 Fujita Kanko, Hakone Hotel Kowakien　ホテル／パンフレット　Hotel/Pamphlet　1992　CD, CW: 小沼謙太郎 Kentaro Konuma　AD, D: 笠島まなぶ Manabu Kasashima　DF: ㈱クーカバーラ Kookaburra

鷺の湯 Sagi no Yu 旅館/パンフレット　Japanese inn/Pamphlet　1995　CD, CW: 阿倍正行 Masayuki Abe　AD, D: 神村 潔 Kiyoshi Kamimura　P: 小南善彦 Yoshihiko Kominami

旅館さかや Ryokan Sakaya 旅館/パンフレット Japanese inn/Pamphlet 1995 CD, AD, D: 宇都宮理人 Masato Utsunomiya P: 伊藤 剛 Tsuyoshi Ito I: 庄司美紀子 Mikiko Shoji CW: 杉浦 諟 Mitomu Sugiura

屋上庭園 Roof Garden

せんせん貴賓特別室 Suite Room

せんせん貴賓特別室専用露天風呂 Open-air Bath

せんせん客室(ツイン) Twin Room

ティーラウンジ「こがり」 Tea Lounge

お土産コーナー「温故のれん」 Souvenir Shop

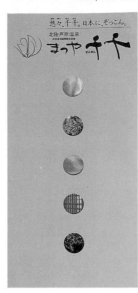

殿方浴場 Men's Grand Bath

男性洗い場 Washing Corner

男性サウナ室 Sauna

男女露天風呂 Open-air Bath

御婦人大浴場 Ladies Grand Bath

一度に300名様がご利用可能。
湯情を高める、石と瓦張りのアプローチ。

26㎡×11㎡、豪華に薫り立つ総檜の天井。

檜の湯縁で出来た幅50㎡×落差4段の滝。

雄大に流れ落ちる幅50m×落差4段の滝。

男女を気にせず使える、独立式の洗い場。

周囲を気にせず使える、ジャクジー＆サウナ風呂。

自然と出来た雄大なジャクジー風呂。

デラックスな女性専用化粧コーナー。

北陸随一のスケール、
木と石をふんだんに使った
500坪の大浴場。

男女脱衣室 Dressing Room

女性専用化粧コーナー Dressing Table

遊び、せんせん。
ゆとり、せんせん。

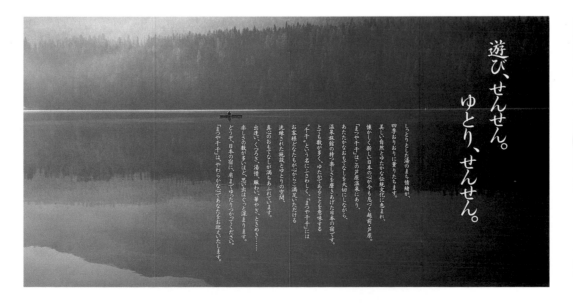

1. まつや 千千 Matsuya Sensen 旅館／パンフレット Japanese inn/Pamphlet 1995 AD, D: 中山由美子 Yumiko Nakayama P: 沼崎 登 Noboru Numasaki CW: 大波加光男 Mitsuo Ohaka
   DF: ㈱バルデザイングループ VAL Design Group Co., Ltd.

2. まつや 千千 Matsuya Sensen 旅館／オープン案内パンフレット Japanese inn/Opening announcement pamphlet 1994 AD, D: 中山由美子 Yumiko Nakayama P: 吉尾正洋 Masahiro Yoshio CW: 大波加光男 Mitsuo Ohaka
   DF: ㈱バルデザイングループ VAL Design Group Co., Ltd.

華
HANA

景
HIROGARI

宵
KOYOI

閑
SHIZUKA

湯
NUKUMORI

華
HANA

TAKAYAMASO
HANANO

高山荘華野 Hanano Takayamaso　旅館／オープン案内パンフレット　Japanese inn/Opening announcement pamphlets　1993　CD: 藤原一宏 Kazuhiro Fujiwara　AD: 三部不二子 Fujiko Sanbe　D: 山口由香子 Yukako Yamaguchi

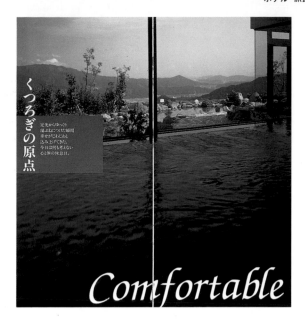

1. 北郷フェニックスリゾート Kitago Phoenix Resort Co., Ltd.　ホテル/パンフレット　Hotel/Pamphlet　1994　CD, AD: 松原祥子 Sachiko Matsubara　D: 塩見 暁 Akira Shiomi　P: 高野典範 Michinori Takano　CW: 日高由美 Yumi Hidaka
　　DF: トッパンアイデアセンター西日本 Toppan Idea Center Nishinippon
2. ホテルリゾネックス名護 Hotel Resonex Nago　ホテル/パンフレット　Hotel/Pamphlet　1994

1. ねざめホテル Nezame Hotel 旅館/パンフレット Japanese inn/Pamphlet 1993 DF: ㈱共立プランニング Kyoritz Planning Corporation

2. 緑水荘 Ryokusuiso 旅館/パンフレット Japanese inn/Pamphlet

1. 湯布院ほてい屋 Yufuin Hoteiya 旅館/パンフレット Japanese inn/Pamphlet 1994 CD: 高木義勝 Yoshikatsu Takagi AD, D: 山口由香子 Yukako Yamaguchi P: 松永勝行 Katsuyuki Matsunaga

2. 山香荘 Yamagaso 旅館/パンフレット Japanese inn/Pamphlet 1994 DF: 西岡スタジオ Nishioka Studio

1. 清光園 Seikoen　旅館/パンフレット　Japanese inn/Pamphlet 1993 DF: 伸 企画 Shin Kikaku

2. 恵ホテル（おんやど恵）Megumi Hotel（Onyado Megumi）旅館/パンフレット　Japanese inn/Pamphlet 1990 DF: ビジュアルアートセンター Visual Art Center

3. だいこく館 Daikokukan　旅館/パンフレット　Japanese inn/Pamphlet 1994 CD, AD, D: 宇都宮理人 Masato Utsunomiya P: 木村浩之 Hiroyuki Kimura

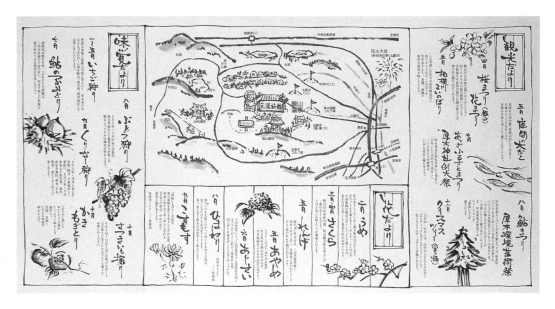

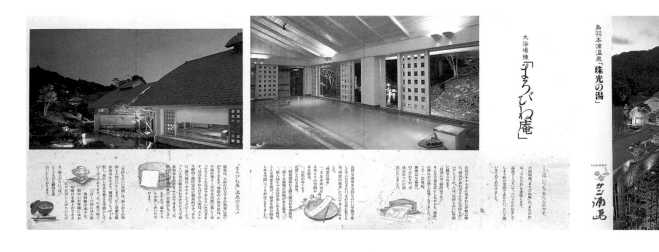

1. 元湯旅館 Motoyu Ryokan　旅館／パンフレット　Japanese inn/Pamphlet 1993　AD, D: 時田勇都 Hayato Tokita　P: 伊藤 剛 Tsuyoshi Ito　CW: 黒木孝宏 Takahiro Kuroki　DF: エイエイピー小田原支店 AAP Odawara Br.
Planning: 山本真司 Shinji Yamamoto

2. 元湯旅館 Motoyu Ryokan　旅館／パンフレット　Japanese inn/Pamphlet 1993　AD, D, I: 黒柳裕子 Yuko Kuroyanagi　CW: 河合美紀 Miki Kawai　DF: エイエイピー小田原支店 AAP Odawara Br.　Planning: 山崎 了 Ryo Yamazaki

3. サン浦島 Sun Urashima　旅館／施設案内パンフレット　Japanese inn/Facilities pamphlet 1994　CD: 池田憲一 Kenichi Ikeda　AD, D, I: 古川直子 Naoko Furukawa　P: 中野充三 Juzo Nakano

1. 宮田観光ホテル 松雲閣 Miyoda Kanko Hotel Shouunkaku 旅館/パンフレット　Japanese inn/Pamphlet　1994　DF: ㈱AAP浜松支店 AAP Hamamatsu Shiten

2. 難波グランドホテル はぎのや 旅館/パンフレット　Japanese inn/Pamphlet　1994　CD, CW: 福士成司 Seiji Fukushi　AD, D: 塩谷利恵子 Rieko Shioya　P: プロフィックス Prophix/久保田昌義 Masayoshi Kubota
DF: ㈱エイエイビー新潟支店 Ad Art Planninng, Co., Ltd. Niigata Br.

1. 坐漁荘 Zagyoso 旅館/パンフレット　Japanese inn/Pamphlet　1985　DF: エイエイビー 三島 A. A. P. Mishima

2. ホテル坂戸城 Hotel Sakatojo 旅館/パンフレット　Japanese inn/Pamphlet　1994　CD, CW: 福士成司 Seiji Fukushi　AD, D: 塩谷利恵子 Rieko Shioya　P: 木村浩之 Hiroyuki Kimura　I: シール Seal/庄司美紀子 Mikiko Shoji
　DF: ㈱エイエイビー新潟支店 AAP Ad Art Plannning, Co., Ltd. Niigata Br.

仙郷楼 Senkyoro 旅館/パンフレット Japanese inn/Pamphlet 1991 CD: 木内正浩 Masahiro Kiuchi AD, D: 渡辺晴美 Harumi Watanabe P: 伊藤 剛 Tsuyoshi Ito/辻満芳雄 Yoshio Tsujima CW: 木内正浩 Masahiro Kiuchi
DF: エイエイビー小田原支店 AAP Odawara Br. Planning: 須田紀也 Toshiya Suda

瀧波 Takinami　旅館/パンフレット　Japanese inn/Pamphlet　1993　AD, D: 星澤初美 Hatsumi Hoshizawa　P: モノリス Monoris/ニュープレス New Press　CW: 萱場由起 Yuki Kayaba

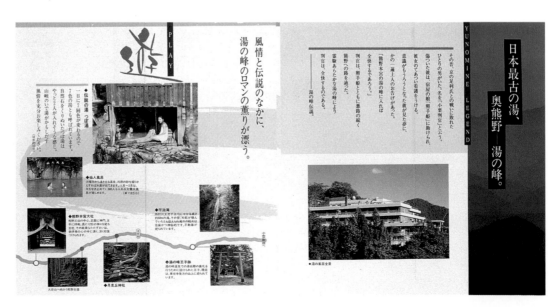

1. 三笠屋 Mikasaya 旅館/総合案内パンフレット Japanese inn/General information pamphlet 1994 CD: 高木義勝 Yoshikastu Takagi AD, D: 三部不二子 Fujiko Sanbe P: 瀧本和人 Kazuto Takimoto CW: 二村志保 Shiho Futamura

2. 湯の峯荘 Yunomineso 旅館/パンフレット Japanese inn/Pamphlet 1993

男と女
いい旅の秘密

ふと、心がなごんだときに思い出す旅のシーン。そんなシーンをたくさん持っているひとは、きっと、いい旅をしている。そして、素敵な—シーンがたくさんあれば、旅ごころがムズムズとまた動き出す。旅は、もう特別なものじゃなくて、私たちのくらしに欠かせないもの。だから、気ままにふらっと出かけよう、いい旅へ。何度も思い出せる素敵なシーンを見つけに—。いい旅には、秘密がある。

INATORISO

CONTENTS

休日は、伊豆にいます。

男女
いい旅の秘密

［男同士の旅］

旅で、男はもりあがる

大漁の笑顔
（平日・休日のみの限定プラン）

特典

① 宴会時飲み放題。（120分）
② 宴会時コンパニオン又は芸妓付。（120分）
③ 二次会もお任せ！
④ お部屋用とおやすみ用に浴衣を二枚ご用意いたします。

おまかせパックⅠ・Ⅱ・Ⅲ全部あわせて
お1人様 25,500円

おまかせパックⅠ
飲み放題
（120分）

おまかせパックⅡ
コンパニオン又は芸妓
（120分）

おまかせパックⅢ
二次会

［女同士の旅］

20代の貴女におくる

淑女の休日
（平日のみの限定プラン）

特典

① 「バー・リブル」で二次会をお楽しみいただけます。（ワンドリンク付）
② お部屋用とおやすみ用に浴衣を二枚ご用意いたします。
③ SPECIAL BREAKFAST 朝食は、洋食・和食をお選びいただけます。
④ チェックイン14時、チェックアウト11時のゆったりプラン。

2 名様	20,000円
3 名様	18,000円
4 名様	16,000円

旅で、女はキレイになる

Special Breakfast

［ゆとりの旅］

旅は、ぜいたくに

四季・女将の献立
（1日5組、平日・休日のみの限定プラン）

特典

① ウェルカムドリンクにてお出迎え。
② ご夕食時に「女将の心遣いひざかけ」をプレゼント。
③ お部屋でゆったりくつろげる部屋帯と浴衣を二枚ご用意いたします。
④ チェックイン14時、チェックアウト11時のゆったりプラン。

2 名様	28,000円
3 名様	24,000円
4 名様	21,000円

女将

いなとり荘 Inatoriso　旅館／パンフレット　Japanese inn/Pamphlet　CD: 山本房史 Fusashi Yamamoto　AD: 時田勇都 Hayato Tokita

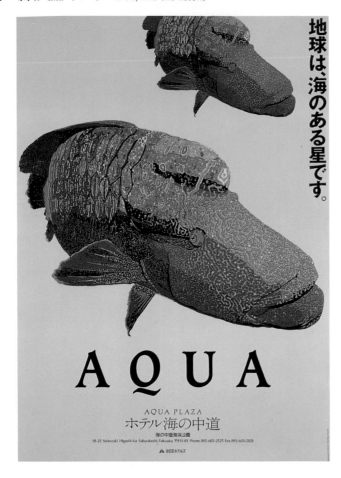

・ ホテル海の中道 Hotel Uminonakamichi　ホテル/ポスター　Hotel/Posters 1990-93　CD, AD: 市川敏明 Toshiaki Ichikawa　D: 後藤敬一 Kazuyuki Goto　I: 水戸丘鋭治 Eiji Mitooka　CW: 市川美野里 Minori Ichikawa
DF: ㈱市川事務所 Office Ichikawa

1. 京都ホテル Kyoto Hotel　ホテル/オープン案内ポスター　Hotel/Opening announcement poster 1994 CD, CW: 赤井 宏 Hiroshi Akai CD: 福井健二 Kenji Fukui AD: 中野直樹 Naoki Nakano/宮本庄二 Shoji Miyamoto
　 D: 林 泰宏 Yasuhiro Hayashi P: 千葉正夫 Masao Chiba CW: 石松かおり Kaori Ishimatsu DF: 中野直樹広告事務所 Naoki Nakano Advertising Office

2. 京都ホテル Kyoto Hotel　ホテル/オープン案内ポスター　Hotel/Opening announcement poster 1994 CD: 赤井 宏 Hiroshi Akai CD: 福井健二 Kenji Fukui AD: 中野直樹 Naoki Nakano/宮本庄二 Shoji Miyamoto D: 安村厚子 Atsuko Yasumura
　 P: 秋元 茂 Shigeru Akimoto CW: 石松かおり Kaori Ishimatsu DF: 中野直樹広告事務所 Naoki Nakano Advertising Office

Front

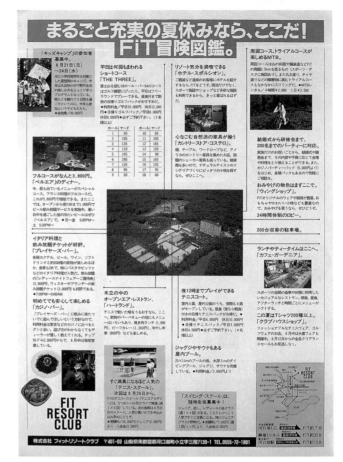

Back

フィットリゾートクラブ FiT RESORT CLUB　リゾート/情報ペーパー、ニュースレター　Resort/Information news-sheet, Newsletter 1994 CD: ㈱フィットリゾートクラブ FiT RESORT CLUB Inc.

■　PACKAGE TOURS　パッケージツアー　■

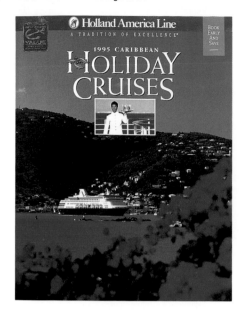

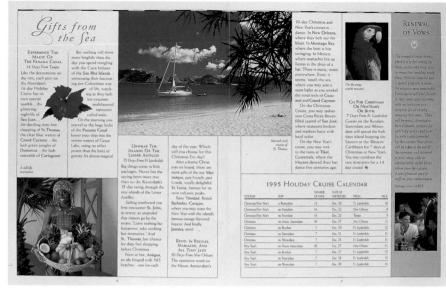

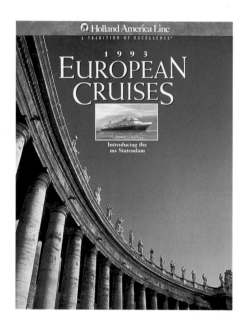

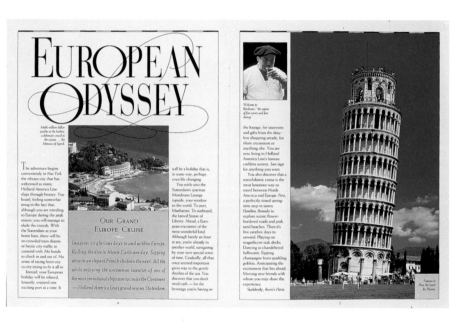

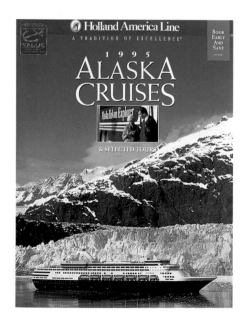

1. **Holland America Line-Westours**　クルーズ会社/パンフレット　Cruise line/Pamphlet　1994　AD, D: John Hornall　D: Paula Cox　CW: Joan Brown　DF: Hornall Anderson Design Works

2. **Holland America Line-Westours**　クルーズ会社/パンフレット　Cruise line/Pamphlet　1992　AD, D: John Hornall　D: Mary Hermes/Kathleen O'Connor　I: John Fretz　CW: Joan Brown　DF: Hornall Anderson Design Works

3. **Holland America Line-Westours**　クルーズ会社/パンフレット　Cruise line/Pamphlet　1994　AD, D: John Hornall　D: Kathleen O'Connor　I: Rolf Goetzinger　CW: Rachel Bard　DF: Hornall Anderson Design Works

PACIFIC IMPRESSIONS

Somewhere in Royal Viking Line's Pacific Rim, old men are taking their songbirds for a walk. Cousins greet each other with prayerful hands and infants are protected from the impure earth because their souls are believed to be close to heaven. We are going to a garden to taste lily flower tea. We are searching for celadon in a shade called "sky blue after rain." We are walking alone through a courtyard built for ninety thousand and we are waiting there for you.

In early 1993, the Royal Viking Queen will sail the Pacific to the world's most populous country, its largest archipelago and its most storied monuments. In ten cruises ranging from the Great Barrier Reef to the Great Wall, from East Africa to the East Indies, the world's most elegant cruise vessel will explore the Pacific Rim in greater depth — and with more style and grace — than ever before.

This is a timeless landscape of thousand-year-old temples and rice terraces worked in the same careful manner since even books can remember. It is a land measured by the rising sun, the passage of dynasties, the chants of monks in saffron robes whose eyes look on eternity.

Come with us to the Pacific of the present, and you come with the scholars and experts who can illuminate the world's most diverse and exotic cultures: the history of China's dragon throne, the politics of Asia's emerging "four dragon" economies, the biological believe-it-or-not of Indonesia's surviving Komodo dragon. With us you will join two decades of experience in Pacific cruising and a staff for which service is an art. But most of all, best of all, you'll join a community of travelers who come not only to see, but to taste, touch, experience and understand what it is in these strange and wonderful lands that drew you to them in the first place.

Caviar is home to tropical birds in Madebui inlet... previous casto forests and the celebrated black marlin. Beyond its shores dolmens the aquatic species of the 1,200-mile Great Barrier Reef, the largest structure in the world made by living creatures.

THE SPLENDORS OF THE MIDDLE KINGDOM One fifth of humanity lives here in a culture that was old when Marco Polo walked across Asia to find it. Two thousand years before Shakespeare wrote, Confucius and Lao-tzu conveyed wisdoms that survive today. Lacquer painting was an art in China when Nineveh was being built, and Rome was still comparing Italy when Chuang-tzu wrote: "I do not know whether I was then a man dreaming I was a butterfly, or whether I am now a butterfly dreaming I am a man."

The Royal Viking Queen will sample the best of China's sights and cities. In Beijing, its famous attractions come alive: the Temple of Heaven, the Great Wall, the Forbidden City and the Summer Palace. In Shanghai you'll dock within sight of the bustling Huangpu River, and the colonial French Quarter still intact behind walls. Buddha, they say, caused flowers to rain from the sky amid the Purple Mountains of Nanjing. In Dalian, antique shops with Russian, Japanese and Chinese artifacts reflect the area's successive rulers. And everywhere in China, proud parents will hold their children up for you to see, thinking, quite correctly, that the simple treasures of family will be the highlight of your visit.

For the Chinese, calligraphy, painting, poetry and music are intimately related, and the treasures of this thriving culture are delightfully diverse...

PACIFIC IMPRESSIONS

Q ROYAL VIKING QUEEN

Come sail in intimate splendor as the Royal Viking Queen explores the cultural richness of the Pacific Rim.

ROYAL VIKING LINE

IN THE LANDS OF ENCHANTMENT Indonesia is the Malay Archipelago — more than 13,000 islands scattered across the equator — which lures visitors with landscapes of green rice paddies, talcum beaches, coral reefs alive with aquatic life, rain forests and unspoiled hillsides. In Borobudur, you'll find an eighth-century Buddhist monument, while Bali beckons with stone temples, gong and gamelan, the grace of a Balinese dance and the artful beauty of batik.

If Bali is serenity, then Bangkok is sensory spice. The golden temples of the city glitter beyond the floating markets on the klong. Breakfast one morning at the venerable Oriental Hotel; sit out on the terrace and regard the Chao Phraya River as it flows by. You're in good company — Graham Greene and William Somerset Maugham left their marks here.

The Royal Viking Queen stays overnight, giving you an opportunity to sample the pleasures of Bangkok-by-night, from traditional Thai dancing at the National Theatre to the dinner of Patpong Road.

In Japan, the Kagoshima countryside offers volcanoes, steaming hot springs and icy crater lakes. Scenic cliffs plunge to the sea at nearby Nagasaki. And in Korea, the truce tables at P'anmunjom and the landing beaches of Inchon are attractions outside Seoul — capital city for more than five centuries.

(Far right) Feel yourself being captivated by a young kayang dancer in Bali; greet your guides near Kagoshima's Nanchu Shrine; pause in front of a temple or stroll the Bird Market in Indonesia's historic Yogyakarta. A procession of Buddhist monks, flowers in hand, file silently into a nearby Bangkok temple.

Royal Viking Line クルーズ会社／パンフレット　Cruise line/Pamphlet　1992-93　CD, AD: Neil Shakery　D: Michael Brosky　CW: Peterson, Skolnick & Dodge　DF: Pentagram Design

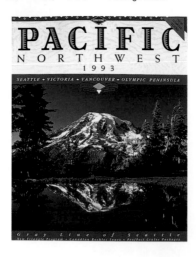

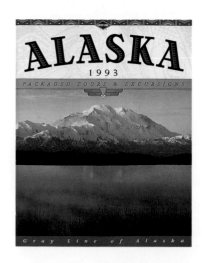

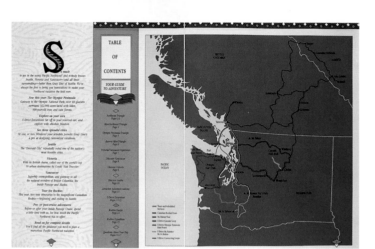

1. **Grayline Tours** ツアー会社/パンフレット　Tour company/Pamphlet　1992　AD, D: John Hornall　D: Heidi Favour　I: Hornall Anderson Design Works　CW: Rachel Bard　DF: Hornall Anderson Design Works

2. **Grayline Tours** ツアー会社/パンフレット　Tour company/Pamphlet　1992　AD, D: John Hornall　D: Heidi Favour/Mary Hermes　I: Tad Wada/HADW　DF: Hornall Anderson Design Works

Royal Viking Line クルーズ会社/パンフレット Cruise line/Pamphlet 1992 CD, AD: Kit Hinrichs D: Jackie Foshaug P: Sherley Busch/Jock McDonald/Bob Esparza/Torry Heffernan I: Ed Lindlf/Dugald Etermor/Teresa Fasolino
CW: Peterson, Skolnick & Dodge DF: Pentagram Design

*H*as the true purpose of travel
remained just beyond your reach?

Royal Viking Line クルーズ会社／パンフレット Cruise line/Pamphlet 1992 CD, AD: Joel Fuller AD, D: Mark Cantor AD, D: Claudia De Castro P: Harvey Lloyd I: Ralf Schuetz CW: Frank Cunningham DF: Pinkhaus Design Corp.

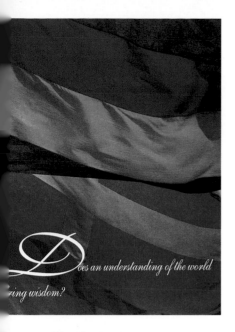

Does an understanding of the world bring wisdom?

hile it is possible to become accustomed to, and even take for granted, the extraordinary shipboard service and cuisine, the Royal Viking Spa will always provide memorable experiences. From stimulating fitness classes to complexion care, mud-packs and massages, the Spa caters to your sense of physical well-being. Ashore, you can go shopping in the fashion capitals of the world. There is an undeniable cachet to buying your Chanel handbag from the designer's Paris store, or having your bespoke boots crafted by Lobb's of London. The treasures you return with may be colorful folk-art carvings from Scandinavia or watercolors from Venice, they may be many or few, but the experience itself will have the greatest value. Later, luxuriating in a warm jacuzzi or basking in the afterglow of a workout, you may find, as you bring your attention fully into the present moment, something akin to a state of grace.

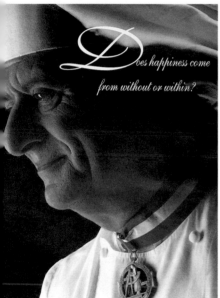

Does happiness come from without or within?

meanwhile, as some are seeking transcendence through the esoteric and others through the everyday, those known as golfers are finding it in the flight of a small white sphere. On select Golf Cruises, professionals from the Golf Digest Instruction Schools are aboard to work with you not only on the physical aspect of the game, but the mental side as well. A perfect golf swing, you may find, is much simpler than you imagine. Ashore, you can take your newfound skills to the historic links of the British Isles and France. Among your treasured memories will be purely struck drives down emerald fairways and pinpoint iron shots into the intimidating greens of the world's most renowned courses.

Our Celebrity Chefs Program brings aboard chefs from the world's leading restaurants to prepare their specialties for you. Paul Bocuse, Guy Legay of the Ritz Hotel in Paris, Alain Ducasse of the Louis XV at the Hotel de Paris, Monte Carlo, and Jeremiah Tower of Stars in San Francisco are among the eminent chefs who may sail with us aboard the Royal Viking Queen.

And the James Beard Foundation will choose award-winning chefs to join us on the Royal Viking Sun. Beyond these superb sensory experiences, this program promises a learning experience as well. Wine makers from Chateaux Lafitte Rothschild will disclose the secrets of the great Bordeaux. And Professor Steve Mutkoski of Cornell University will help you become expert at pairing foods with wine. Perhaps happiness doesn't come from anywhere. It is always simply right here, waiting for you to open yourself to it.

If the pearls of experience are beyond price, how is it they always cost less than they're worth?

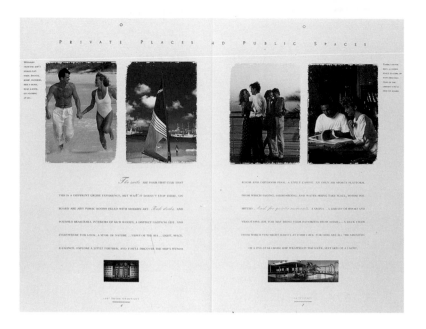

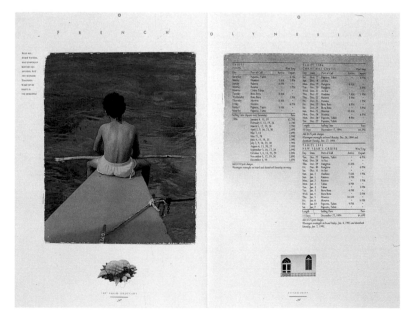

Windstar Cruises　クルーズ会社/パンフレット　Cruise line/Pamphlet　1993　AD, D: Jack Anderson　D: Debra Hampton/Paula Cox/John Anicker/Lian Ng　P: Tom Collicott　I: John Fretz/Bruce Morser/Dean Williams/Todd Connor　CW: Pamela Mason-Davey
DF: Hornall Anderson Design Works

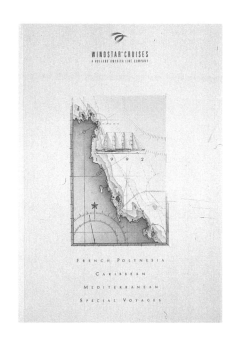

Windstar Cruises クルーズ会社／パンフレット　Cruise line/Pamphlet 1991　AD, D: Jack Anderson　D: Paula Cox/Denise Weir　I: Bruce Morser　CW: Joan Brown　DF: Hornall Anderson Design Works

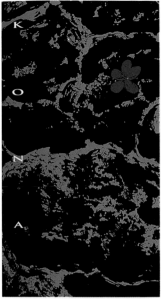

HAWAII
PRO BOWL

MILLER BREWING COMPANY · FEBRUARY 1-5, 1991.

TIME DIFFERENCE When it's noon in Hawaii, it is 3:00 p.m. in Los Angeles...4:00 p.m. in Denver...5:00 p.m. in Chicago and 6:00 p.m. in New York. ✻

NAME BADGE You'll receive your name badge upon checking in at the Miller Masters Hospitality Suite at the Ritz-Carlton. Please wear it to all planned functions throughout the trip to identify yourself to the Travel Staff and fellow guests as a prestigious Miller Master. ✻

TRAVEL STAFF Your Miller Masters Travel Staff will be located in the Plaza III Ballroom of the Ritz-Carlton (just off the main lobby.) If you need information or special assistance during your stay, please do not hesitate to contact your Travel Staff. Changes in the program itinerary, bulletins, messages, etc. will be posted at the desk. Information and sign-ups for all activities will be handled there as well. Your Travel Staff is: Lisa Stewart • Thomas Herget • Brad Hasper • Kathie Johnson • Vince Aspromonte ✻

MILLER MASTERS HOSPITALITY SUITE The Miller Masters Hospitality Suite will be located in the Plaza III Ballroom of the Ritz-Carlton (just off the main lobby.) Feel free to stop by for morning coffee, afternoon or evening refreshments and conversation. Your Travel Staff will always be available to assist you with any special requests. ✻ Hospitality Suite hours are from 7:00 a.m throughout the day, and until midnight following each evening's events.

• 5 •

*A*ll travel arrangements in conjunction with your upcoming trip to the 1991 "Party at the Pro Bowl" in Honolulu have been taken care of by Miller Brewing Company . . . including round-trip transportation, elegant resort accommodations, sightseeing adventures, taxes and gratuities.

Please keep this daily Program of Events handy for reference . . . it details times, places and activities during your stay in Honolulu.

DAY ONE SATURDAY, MAY 18, 1991 ✻ Daytime Dress: Comfortable traveling clothes. ✻ Evening Dress: Casual; slacks and sport shirt, summer dress. Wrap for cool ocean breezes. Flat shoes recommended for women, reception on lawn area. ✻ Miller Masters and guests wing their way toward the Pacific and the idyllic islands of Hawaii! ✻ Important Flight Information: In checking luggage from your home city, be certain your bags are checked all the way through to KONA. Your claim stub should read, "KOA". ✻ Your flight to Kona will be connecting through Honolulu International Airport. When you arrive in Honolulu, make your way to the Inter-Island Air Terminal for your Hawaiian Air or Aloha Air flights. You can either walk to this terminal or take the "wiki wiki" shuttle bus. Upon reaching the Inter-Island Terminal, look for your Miller Masters Travel Staff, holding a "Miller Masters" sign. They will assist you in checking in for your short flight to Kona. ✻ Upon arrival in Kona, you'll be met by your Miller Masters Travel Staff...once again, look for a Miller Masters sign. They will assist you with luggage and transportation to the Ritz-Carlton Mauna Lani (approximately a 20 minute ride.) ✻ NOTE: Due to limited baggage compartments on inter-island flights, luggage is sometimes delayed a flight or two. You may want to pack a swimsuit, cosmetics, etc. in a carry-on in case of such a delay (flights run every hour.) ✻ The fabled Ritz-Carlton lions greet Miller Masters as they pass through the front gates into a world of elegance and beauty. ✻ You'll be greeted at the door and directed to the Miller Masters

• 6 •

DAY THREE
SUNDAY, FEBRUARY 3, 1991

DAYTIME DRESS:
Casual sportswear.
EVENING DRESS:
Casual sportswear.

BREAKFAST — Begin today with a healthy breakfast in the hotel. Please sign the check with your name, room number and "Miller Brewing Company."

Miller Brewing Company "Party at the Pro Bowl" incentive winners enjoy breakfast at leisure in the hotel prior to departing for the game. Again, please sign the check with your name, room number and "Miller Brewing Company."

11:00 A.M. Miller Brewing Company "Party at the Pro Bowl" incentive winners gather on Koa Avenue (located on the first floor behind the main building) for transfer to Aloha Stadium. At the stadium, enjoy a tailgate party, complete with barbeque, pre-game show and Miller products.

3:00 P.M. The 1991 "Party at the Pro Bowl" Game begins . . . Miller Brewing Company "Party at the Pro Bowl" incentive winners enjoy great seats, a full-color game program and variety of game essentials like sunglasses and suntan lotion!

IMPORTANT: PLEASE REMEMBER WHERE YOUR MILLER BREWING COMPANY COACH IS PARKED AND MAKE YOUR WAY BACK TO THE COACH IMMEDIATELY FOLLOWING THE GAME!

7:00 P.M.–9:00 P.M. Miller Brewing Company "Party at the Pro Bowl" incentive winners gather at the hotel's Ballroom, located in the Convention Center, for a "Victory Celebration." Enjoy your favorite Miller products, dinner-style hors d'oeuvres and game highlights.

MILLER BREWING COMPANY'S HOSPITALITY DESK HOURS ARE 8:00 A.M.–11:00 A.M.

1. **The Masters Group** 社内旅行パンフレット/Incentire travel schedule 1990 AD, D: Scott Mires DF: Mires Design, Inc.

2. **Miller Brewing/Masters** 社内旅行パンフレット/Incentire travel schedule 1991 AD, D: José Serrano I: Tracy Sabin DF: Mires Design, Inc.

Baja Tours ツアー会社/パンフレット Tour company/Pamphlet 1995 CD, AD, P, CW: Mike Salisbury D: Mary Evezyn/Mc Gouga DF: Mike Salisbury Communications

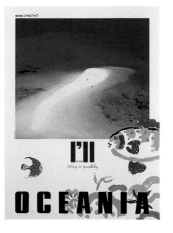

1. ジャルパック Jalpak 旅行代理店/パンフレット Travel agency/Pamphlet 1993 AD: 清水正行 Masayuki Shimizu D: 馬場久美子 Kumiko Baba CW: 佐藤みどり Midori Sato DF: (株)アルファルファ Alfalfa Design Studio

2. 日本航空 Japan Airlines 航空会社/パンフレット Airline/Pamphlet 1993 AD: 清水正行 Masayuki Shimizu D: 馬場久美子 Kumiko Baba CW: 千田 隆 Takashi Senda DF: (株)アルファルファ Alfalfa Design Studio

3. ジャルパック Jalpak 旅行代理店/ポスター Travel agency/Posters 1994 AD: 清水正行 Masayuki Shimizu D: 加賀 裕 Yutaka Kaga I: 中林康広 Yasuhiro Nakabayashi DF: (株)アルファルファ Alfalfa Design Studio

Resorts in Australia

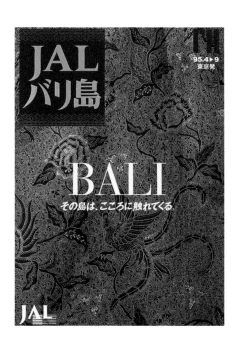

JAMAICA
ミックス・カルチャーが醸し出す ジャマイカン・リゾートの魅力

GRAND PALAZZO
入江の宮殿ホテル

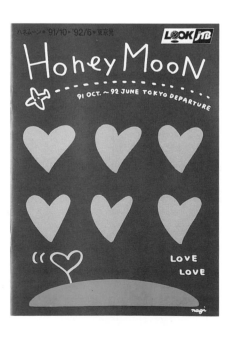

1, 2, 4, 5. JTBワールド JTB World 旅行代理店/パンフレット　Travel agency/Pamphlets 1990-91 DF: ㈱フォルツァート Forzato Co., Ltd. A: JIC （㈱日本交通事業社）　JIC Corporation

3. 日清航空 Nissin Travel Services 旅行代理店/パンフレット　Travel agency/Pamphlets 1992 I: 松原健治 Kenji Matsubara DF: バウ広告事務所 Bau Advertising Office

1
2

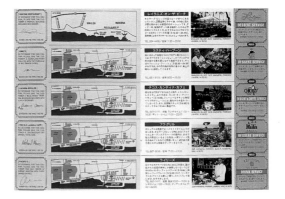

1. ジャルストーリー Jal Story　旅行代理店／パンフレット　Travel agency/Pamphlet 1995 CD: 池谷芳幸 Yoshiyuki Ikegaya AD: 桶谷達也 Tatsuya Oketani D: 西村哲矢 Tetsuya Nishimura P: 安斎 肇 Hajime Anzai
CW: 田森むつみ Mutsumi Tamori DF: 中央宣興㈱ Chuo Senko Advertising Co., Ltd.

2. 日本航空 Japan Airlines　航空会社／クーポンブック　Airline/Discount coupon booklet 1995 CD: 神宮章嘉 Akiyoshi Jingu AD: 清水正行 Masayuki Simizu D: 加賀 裕 Yutaka Koga/遠藤恵子 Keiko Endo
DF: ㈱アルファルファ Alfalfa Design Studio

1. 全日空ワールド ANA World Tours 旅行代理店／パンフレット　Travel agency/Pamphlet　1995

2, 3, 4. 全日空ワールド ANA World Tours 旅行代理店／パンフレット　Travel agency/Pamphlets　1995

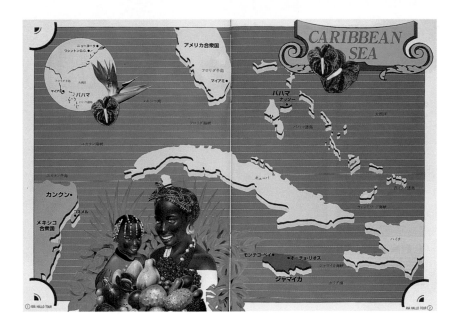

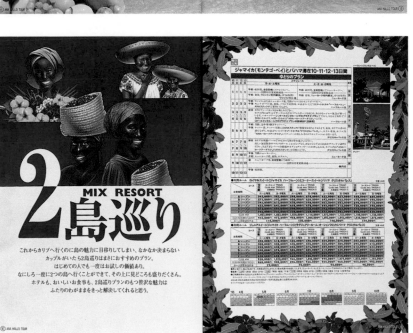

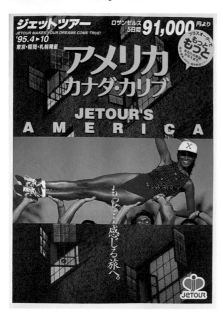

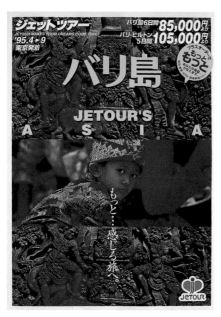

プレイガイド トラベル Playguide Tours　旅行代理店/パンフレット　Travel agency/Pamphlets　1995　D: 駒形祐美子 Yumiko Komagata　CW: 菊池友子 Tomoko Kikuchi/瀬戸隆太 Ryuta Seto

1. 東日本旅客鉄道 East Japan Railways 旅客鉄道会社/パンフレット Rail company/Pamphlet 1994 CD, AD, D: 木下勝弘 Katsuhiro Kinoshita P: 大橋 力 Tsutomu Ohashi

2, 3. JR西日本 West Japan Railways 旅客鉄道会社/ポスター Rail company/Posters 1991 CD, AD: 畑 美治 Yoshiharu Hata AD: 中野直樹 Naoki Nakano D: 太田 隆 Takashi Ota/越智正二 Masashi Ochi P: 萩原佳一 Yoshikazu Hagiwara

I: ワークス Works CW: 清水清春 Kiyoharu Shimizu DF: 中野直樹広告事務所 Naoki Nakano Advertising Office A: 東急エージェンシー関西支社 Tokyu Agency Kansai Branch

1, 2. ヴィータ VITA 旅行代理店／パンフレット Travel agency/Pamphlets 1994

3, 4. ミリオンパック Million-Pack 旅行代理店／チラシ Travel agency/Flyers 1990 I: 田中ひろみ Hiromi Tanaka

5, 6. ジェイエイエス商事 JAS Trading & Travel 旅行代理店／パンフレット Travel agency/Pamphlets 1995 AD: 八島 建 Takeru Yashima D: 中村明彦 Akihiko Nakamura ／ 石井和浩 Kazuhiro Ishii I: 升 たか Taka Masu
CW: 矢原政徳 Masanori Yahara DF: ㈱アドバタイズ Advertise

1. 小田急トラベルサービス ODAKYU Travel Service　旅行代理店／パンフレット　Travel agency/Pamphlet 1995 CD, P: 今井輝光 Terumitsu Imai AD, D: 堀美善子 Misako Hori CW: 小倉 淳 Atsushi Ogura

2. オリオンツアー Orion Tour　旅行代理店／パンフレット　Travel agency/Pamphlet 1995 CD: 野谷秀子 Hideko Notani AD: 鈴木 隆 Takashi Suzuki D: 椿 恵美 Emi Tsubaki CW: 西村久美子 Kumiko Nishimura
   DF: ㈱コンセプトアーツ Concept Art Co., Ltd./DEWクリエイティブ DEW Creative

3. 日本交通公社 Japan Travel Bureau　旅行代理店／ポスター　Travel agency/Poster 1994 AD: 池田 敦 Atsushi Ikeda P: 田辺裕晶 Hiroaki Tanabe P: 山崎博文 Hirofumi Yamazaki CW: 川島英司 Eiji Kawashima DF: 第一製版㈱ Daiichi Printing Co.

4. オリオンツアー Orion Tour　旅行代理店／パンフレット　Travel agency/Pamphlet 1995 AD, D: 小田島亜古 Ako Kodashima I: 波岡郁子 Ikuko Namioka DF: ㈲ヴィコラージュ V. Collage

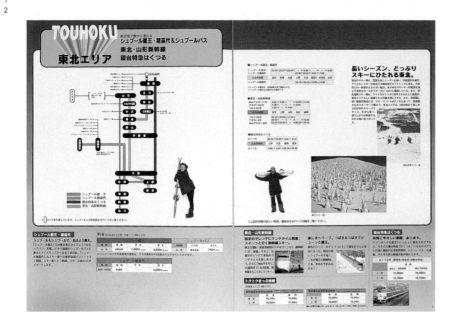

1. 東日本旅客鉄道 East Japan Railway 旅客鉄道会社／パンフレット　Rail company／Pamphlet　P: 若月 勤 Tsutomu Wakatsuki

2. 東日本旅客鉄道 East Japan Railway 旅客鉄道会社／パンフレット　Rail company／Pamphlet　CD: 伊東俊幸 Toshiyuki Ito　AD: 小林 稔 Minoru Kobayashi　CW: 佐藤優巳 Masami Sato　DF: リクルート Recruit

1. 東急観光 Tokyu Tourist 旅行代理店/パンフレット Travel agency/Pamphlet AD: 宮本英男 Hideo Miyamoto D: 高野眞逸六 Shinichiro Takano CW: 藤井雅幸 Masayuki Fujii DF: トーワクリエイティブ㈱ Towa Creative Inc.

2. 小笠原海運 Ogasawara Kaiun 海運会社/パンフレット Shipping company/Pamphlet 1994 DF: RED刷 R Printing

1. ジャルストーリー **Jal Story** 旅行代理店／パンフレット　Travel agency/Pamphlet　1995　CD: 山田裕一 Yuichi Yamada　AD: 村松行雄 Yukio Muramatsu　CW: 北條かおる Kaoru Hojo　DF: マックスデザイン事務所 Mcs Design Studio

2. 全日空商事 **ANA Trading** 旅行代理店／パンフレット　Travel agency/Pamphlet　1995

1, 2, 3. 東日本旅客鉄道 East Japan Railway 旅客鉄道会社/パンフレット　Rail company/Pamphlets 1995

4. 東日本旅客鉄道 East Japan Railway 旅客鉄道会社/パンフレット　Rail company/Pamphlet　CD: 伊東俊幸 Toshiyuki Ito　AD: 研 文也 Fumiya Ishii　D: 浅古 恵 Megumi Asako　DF: コーレー㈱ Coray Co.

5. 東日本旅客鉄道 East Japan Railway 旅客鉄道会社/パンフレット　Rail company/Pamphlet　CD: 伊東俊幸 Toshiyuki Ito　AD: 高橋和義 Kazuyoshi Takahashi　DF: 高木デザイン事務所 Takagi Design Office

6. 日本旅行 Nihon Ryoko 旅行代理店/パンフレット　Travel agency/Pamphlet 1994　CD: 高田 篤 Atsushi Takada　AD, D: 五十嵐昭好 Akiyoshi Igarashi

7. 農協観光 Nokyo Kanko 旅行代理店/パンフレット　Travel agency/Pamphlet 1991　CD: 辻本良雄 Yoshio Tsujimoto　AD, D: 山田伸治 Nobuharu Yamada　P: (スタジオ・ドーメン) 家中泰義 Studio Domen, Yasuyoshi Ienaka
I: 中島万智子 Machiko Nakajima　CW: 岩崎泰三 Taizo Iwasaki

1. 藤田観光 Fujita Kanko ホテル、リゾート運営会社/ポスター Hotel & resort development company/Poster 1994 AD, D: 富川まゆみ Mayumi Tomikawa P: 草月アートプランニング SOGETSU A. P.　CW: 小沼謙太郎 Kentaro Konuma
　DF: (株)クーカバーラ Kookaburra

2. 箱根小涌園 Hakone Kowakien ホテル/ポスター Hotel/Poster 1994 CD: 田中公仁郎 Kojiro Tanaka AD: 長谷川義乗 Yoshinori Hasegawa D: 佐藤康子 Yasuko Sato CW: 山添浩太郎 Kotaro Yamazoe

3. 藤田観光 Fujita Kanko ホテル、リゾート運営会社/ポスター Hotel & resort development company/Poster 1994 CD, CW: 小沼謙太郎 Kentaro Konuma AD, D: 山崎美穂 Miho Yamazaki P: 金子正明 Masaaki Kaneko
　DF: (株)クーカバーラ Kookaburra

4. 藤田観光 Fujita Kanko ホテル、リゾート運営会社/ポスター Hotel & resort development company/Poster 1992 CD: 小沼謙太郎 Kentaro Konuma AD, D: 山崎美穂 Miho Yamazaki I: みやもとえつよし Etsuyoshi Miyamoto
　CW: 山家一男 Kazuo Yanbe DF: (株)クーカバーラ Kookaburra

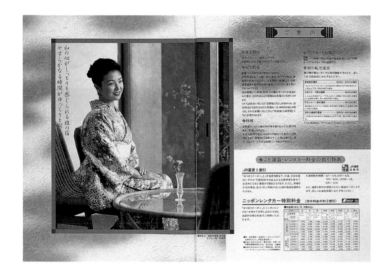

東急観光 Tokyu Tourist 旅行代理店 /パンフレット　Travel agency/Pamphlets　CD, CW: 松本加代 Kayo Matsumoto　AD, D: 池内基郎 Motoo Ikeuchi　P: 杉山栄紘 Eiko Sugiyama　DF: ㈱東急エージェンシー Tokyu Agency Inc.

1. JR東日本 秋田支社 East Japan Railways, Akita Branch 旅客鉄道会社/パンフレット Rail company/Pamphlets 1993 AD, D: 工藤こう子 Koko Kudo CW: 播磨屋誠次 Seiji Harimaya

2, 3, 4. 日本旅行 Nippon Travel Agency 旅行代理店/パンフレット Travel agency/Pamphlets 1995

日本交通公社 Japan Travel Bureau 旅行代理店/ポスター Travel agency/Posters 1994 AD: 池田 敦 Atsushi Ikeda D: 田辺裕晶 Hirooki Tanabe CW: 川島英司 Eiji Kawashima/初海 淳 Jun Hatsuumi DF: 第一製版㈱ Daiichi Printing Co.

■　　TOURIST ATTRACTIONS　観光地　　■

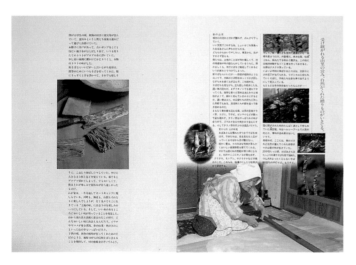

1. 南相木村 Minamiaikimura　パンフレット Pamphlet　1992　CD: ㈱コックス Cox　AD, D, P, I, CW, DF: ㈱アズ Creative Agency Az　P: スタジオ・イソガイ Studio Isogai

2. 十日町市役所商工観光課 Tokamachi City Tourist Bureau　パンフレット Pamphlet　1993　CD: 村山幸男 Yukio Murayama　AD, D: 馬場正樹 Masaki Baba　P: 中澤富雄 Tomio Nakazawa　DF: 三条印刷㈱ Sanjo Printing Co., Ltd.

関金町役場 Sekigane Town　パンフレット　Pamphlet　1990　AD, D, CW: 井上八重美 Yaemi Inoue　DF: ㈲アイ・カンパニー I.Company Inc.

1. **グアム政府観光局 Guam Visitors Bureau** ポスター Poster 1993 CD, CW: ボブ ウォード Bob Ward AD, D: 小山和彦 Kazuhiko Koyama D: 馬場 悟 Satoru Baba P: 相川喜伸 Yoshinobu Ikawa A: 旭通信社 Asatsu Inc.

2. **グアム政府観光局 Guam Visitors Bureau** ポスター Poster 1993 CD, CW: ボブ ウォード Bob Ward AD, D: 小山和彦 Kazuhiko Koyama D: 馬場 悟 Satoru Baba P: 相川喜伸 Yoshinobu Ikawa I: 黒川洋行 Hiroyuki Kurokawa

3, 4. **グアム政府観光局 Guam Visitors Bureau** ポスター Posters 1993 CD, CW: ボブ ウォード Bob Ward AD, D: 小山和彦 Kazuhiko Koyama P: 相川喜伸 Yoshinobu Ikawa DF: 馬場 悟 Satoru Baba A: 旭通信社 Asatsu Inc.

グアム政府観光局 Guam Visitors Bureau ポスター Posters 1994 CD, CW: ボブ ウォード Bob Ward AD, D: 小山和彦 Kazuhiko Koyama P: 佐藤ヒデキ Hideki Satoh DF: 馬場 悟 Satoru Baba

1. 道路施設協会仙台支部 Japan Highway Services Association　ガイドブック　Guide book　1994　CD: 山本 光 Hikaru Yamamoto　AD, D: 桜庭宏明 Hiroaki Sakuraba　I: 大村斗喜子 Tokiko Omura/沖崎一也 Kazuya Okizaki/
庄司美紀子 Mikiko Shoji/鈴木 修 Osamu Suzuki/樽井純夫 Sumio Tarui/本郷けい子 Keiko Hongo/本郷由紀子 Yukiko Hongo　CW: 萱場由起 Yuki Kayaba

2. NTT東北電話帳事業推進部 NTT Tohoku Branch　ガイドブック　Guide book　1995　CD: 山本 光 Hikaru Yamamoto　AD: 房州久美 Kuni Boshu　D: ハートアンドブレーン Heart & Brain　P: フォトスタジオ スクープ Photo Studio Scoop
I: 本郷由紀子 Yukiko Hongo　CW: 萱場由起 Yuki Kayaba

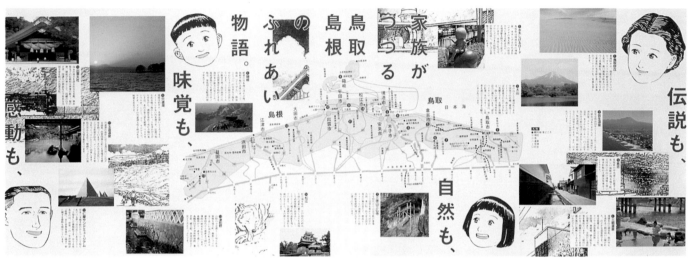

1. 鳥取県，島根県 Tottori & Shimane Prefectures パンフレット Pamphlet 1994 CD: 海嶋達也 Tatsuya Umijima AD: 金井泰浩 Yasuhiro Kanai D: 中藤良枝 Yoshie Nakato I: 谷口ジロー Jiro Taniguchi CW: 佐々木繁和 Shigekazu Sasaki

2. 岡山県 Okayama Prefecture パンフレット Pamphlet 1994 I: わたせせいぞう Seizo Watase

BITCHU DRAMATIC STORY

ドラマの宝石箱。備中。

NATURAL TASTE BITCHU

備中の自然は 三ツ星レストラン。

岡山県高梁地方振興局 Takahashi City パンフレット Pamphlets 1991 DF: ㈱電通岡山支社 Dentsu Inc., Okayama Branch

NATURAL DYNAMISM
森の四季

silent narrators
森の仲間

森町商工観光課 Mori Town Tourist Bureau パンフレット Pamphlet 1994 CD, AD: 島田 実 Minoru Shimada P: 湯山 繁 Shigeru Yuyama/岩田真知 Matomo Iwata CW: 石田たまみ Tamami Ishida

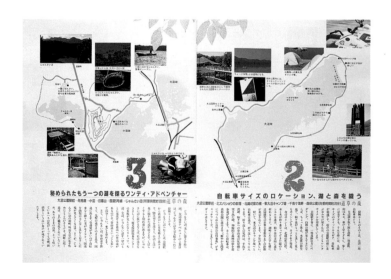

七飯町役場商工観光課 Nanaii Town Tourist Bureau　パンフレット　Pamphlet　1994　CD, AD, D: 鈴木南海男 Namio Suzuki　P: 佐々木郁夫 Ikuo Sasaki　CW: 森 浩義 Hiroyoshi Mori

1. 雄武町 Oumu Town パンフレット Pamphlet

2. 礼文町 Rebun Town パンフレット Pamphlet 1994 AD, D: 鈴木南海雄 Namio Suzuki P: 湯山 繁 Shigeru Yuyama CW: 加藤 玄 Gen Kato DF: ノモスパブリシティ Nomos Publicity

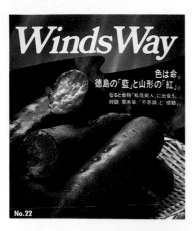

長野県 Nagano Prefecture　パンフレット　Pamphlet　1993　CD, AD, D: 麻生克之 Katsuyuki Aso　I: 山田修史 Shushi Yamada　CW: 麻生光子 Mitsuko Aso

1. 立科町役場 Tateshina Town　パンフレット　Pamphlet　1994
2. 坂北村役場 Sakakita Village　パンフレット　Pamphlet　CD, AD, D: 大橋英彦 Hidehiko Ohashi　P: 海野 勝 Masaru Unno／中沢 勲 Isao Nakazawa　CW: 村松 忍 Shinobu Muramatsu　DF: ㈱エイブル Able　A: ㈱アプラン Apran

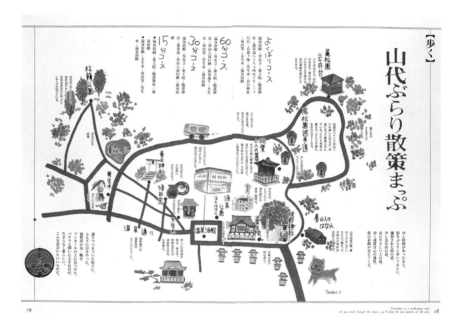

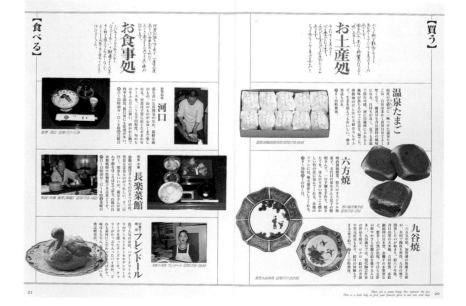

山代温泉観光協会 Yamashiro Hot Spring Tourist Association　情報誌　Information pamphlet 1993-94　CD: 錦織健志 Kenji Nishikori　AD, D, I: 神川ちなみ Chinami Kamikawa　AD, CW: 二村志保 Shiho Futamura　CW: 木本宅治 Takuji Kimoto

山代温泉観光協会 Yamashiro Hot Spring Tourist Association　情報誌 Information pamphlet 1993-94 CD: 錦織健志 Kenji Nishikori AD, D, I: 神川ちなみ Chinami Kamikawa AD, CW: 二村志保 Shiho Futamura CW: 木本宅治 Takuji Kimoto

伊豆山温泉観光協会 Izusan Hot Spring Tourist Association　パンフレット　Pamphlet　CD, AD: 垣野建一 Kenichi Kakino　D: 杉山摂郎 Setsuro Sugiyama　P: 久保田昌義 Masayoshi Kubota　I: 鈴木 真 Makoto Suzuki　CW: 伴 久美子 Kumiko Ban
DF: ㈱エイエイピー　AAP Inc.

越き想い湧きいづる
湖の日々

白山が麗しい湖のまち
片山津温泉

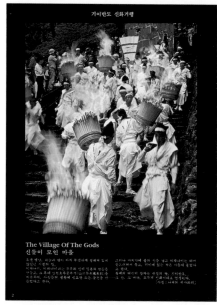

T.A.P紀伊半島実行委員会 Kii Peninsula TAP Executive Commission パンフレット Pamphlet 1994 CD: 海嶋達也 Tatsuya Umijima AD: 岩本 淳 Jun Iwamoto D: 高橋里志 Satoshi Takahashi/崎谷正美 Masami Sakitani
P: 矢野建彦 Takehiko Yano/浅井康弘 Yasuhiro Asai/梅川紀彦 Norihiko Umekawa I: 園家文苑 Bunsen Sonoke CW: 游 春治 Shunji Yu/吉村美香 Mika Yoshimura/ジョン ケプラー John Keppler

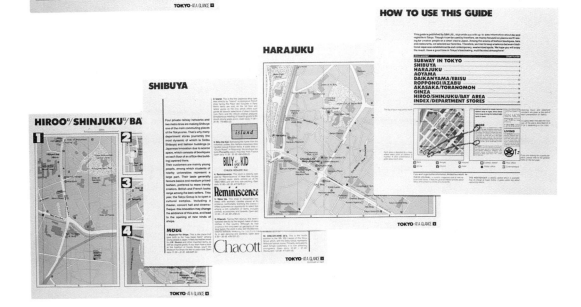

1. エス・ビー・エー SBA クリエイター用東京ガイドブック Specialist Tokyo guide 1989 CD, CW: 田村亜弥 Aya Tamura AD, D: 細山田光宣 Mitsunobu Hosoyamada I: 久保田二雄 Tsugio Kubota/川瀬一雄 Kazuo Kawase DF: ㈱細山田デザイン事務所 Hosoyamada Design Office

2. TIA-Typographers Int'l Association パンフレット Pamphlet CD, AD, D, Cover Photo: Rick Eiber DF: Rick Eiber Design

1. 望月町観光協会 Mochizuki Town Tourist Association パンフレット Pamphlet 1993

2. 鳥取県中部広域行政管理組合 Tottori Prefecture Municipalities Association パンフレット Pamphlet 1991 AD, D, I, CW: 井上八重美 Yaemi Inoue DF: ㈲アイ・カンパニー I. Company Inc.

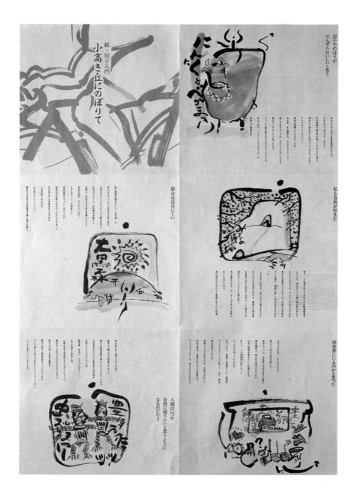

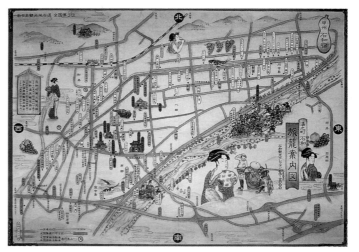

1. 多賀城市 Tagajo City　パンフレット Pamphlet 1994 DF: ㈱ユーメディア U-MEDIA Co., Ltd.

2. 田子町役場（地域振興課）Takko Town　パンフレット Pamphlet 1993 CD, CW: 赤坂 敬 Takashi Akasaka D: 福岡政剛 Seigo Fukuoka P: 小倉賢治 Kenji Ogura I: 斉藤広康 Hiroyasu Saito

3. 石和町商工観光課 Isawa Town Tourist Bureau　マップ Map

1. 岩手県東和町役場 Towa Town　パンフレット　Pamphlet　DF: 川嶋印刷(株) Kawashima Printing

2. 上野観光協会 Ueno City Tourist Association　パンフレット　Pamphlet　1978

3. 別所温泉旅館組合 Bessho Spa　パンフレット　Pamphlet　1992　CD: 別所温泉旅館組合宣伝部 Bessho Spa, Advertising Div.　DF: 竹内印刷 Takeuchi Printing

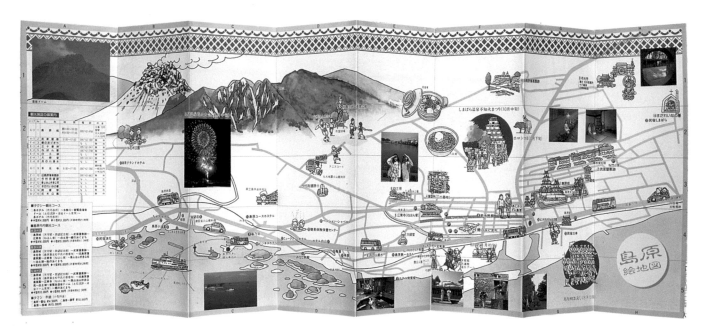

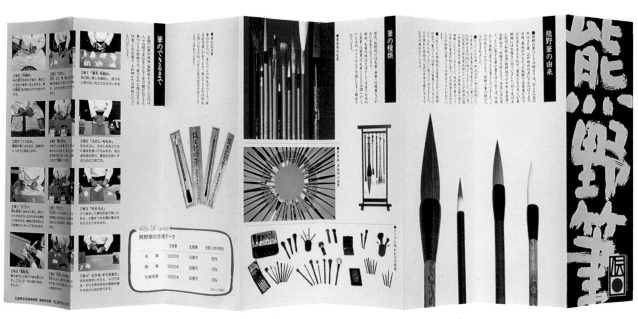

1. 島原市役所 Shimabara City　ガイドマップ　Guide map　1994　CD: 永江圭爾 Keiji Nagae　AD: 吉田文彦 Fumihiko Yoshida　D: 溝上淳一 Junichi Mizokami　P: 西川清人 Kiyoto Nishikawa/林谷 隆 Takashi Hayashiya
　　I: 天野雄二 Yuji Amano　CW: 松崎浩一郎 Koichiro Matsuzaki　DF: トップラン Toplan
2. 熊野町役場 Kumano Town Office　パンフレット　Pamphlet　CD, AD: 藤本嘉元 Yoshiharu Fujimoto　DF: ㈲スタジオアルタ Studio Alta

1. 茨城県観光協会 Ibaragi Prefecture Tourist Association　パンフレット　Pamphlet 1994　DF: 協同広告㈱ Kyodo Advertising Company

2. 金ケ崎町役場 Kanegasaki Town Hall　パンフレット　Pamphlet 1993　DF: 川口印刷工業㈱ Kawaguchi Printing Industry Co., Ltd.

1. 川辺町役場 Kawabe Town パンフレット Pamphlet CD, AD: 田中 正 Tadashi Tanaka D, I, CW: 近藤真規子 Makiko Kondo P: 吉田将夫 Masao Yoshida DF: ㈱都市設計総合研究所

2. 千厩町産業振興課 Senmaya Town パンフレット Pamphlet 1994 DF: 川嶋印刷㈱ Kawashima Printing

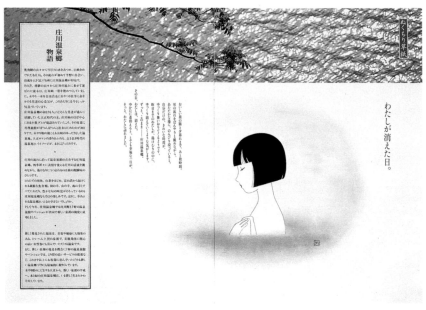

庄川泉源 Shogawa Sengen パンフレット Pamphlet 1992 CD, CW: 高橋修宏 Nobuhiro Takahashi AD: 滝川正弘 Masahiro Takigawa D: 船見尚子 Naoko Funami P: 松本道夫 Michio Matsumoto/赤羽仁諭 Jinyu Akabane
I: 島崎文雄 Fumio Shimazaki DF: ㈲クロス Cross, Inc.

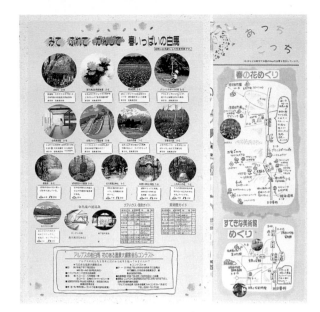

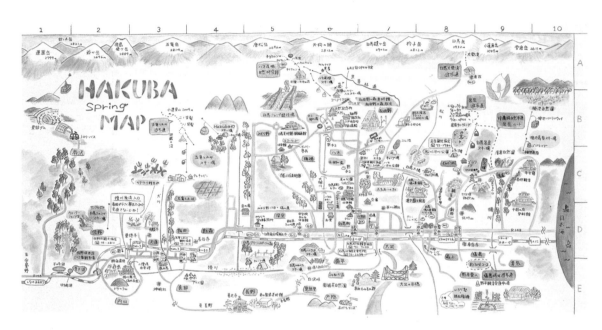

Front

Back

白馬村観光連盟 Hakubamura Tourist Association　マップ、情報ペーパー Map, Information news-sheet 1995 CD: 鈴木孝子 Takako Suzuki AD: 水沢ゆかり Yukari Mizusawa D: 湯本京子 Kyoko Yumoto
DF: ㈱C&Fコミュニケーションズ C&F Communications

お経を唱えるセミがいた。

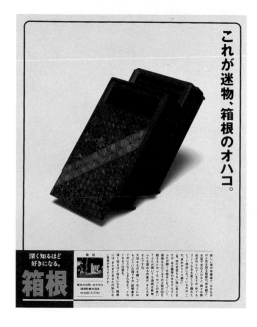

これが迷物、箱根のオハコ。

寿命が七年延びるタマゴ。

晴れ女に逢えたら、いい旅です。

アメリカ生まれの芦ノ湖育ち。

箱根の山に鬼がいた。

箱根町観光協会 Hakone Town Tourist Association　ポスター　Posters 1994　AD, D: 池田 敦 Atsushi Ikeda　D: 本多 集 Tsudou Honda　P: 岡田元伸 Motonobu Okada　CW: 川島英司 Eiji Kawashima

1. 登別観光協会 Noboribetsu Tourist Association　パンフレット Pamphlet 1992 DF: エムツーカンパニー M2 Company

2. 隠岐観光協会 Oki Tourist Association　パンフレット Pamphlet

3, 4. 新見市観光局 Niimi City Tourist Bureau　ポスター Posters 1987 AD, D: 河本文夫 Fumio Kawamoto　P: 千葉正夫 Masao Chiba　CW: 中達玲子 Reiko Nakatatsu　DF: ㈱オフィスカワモト Office Kawamoto Inc.

1, 2. 野沢温泉村 Nozawa Onsen Village　ポスター　Posters　1992-94　CD: 小島正昭 Masaaki Kojima　AD, D: 戸田良久 Yoshihisa Toda　P: 石川英一 Eiichi Ishikawa　CW: 岡部由美子 Yumiko Okabe　DF: 長野デザインセンター Nagano Design Center

3, 4. 大館市役所 Odate City　ポスター　Posters　1990　CD, AD, D: 小畑正博 Masahiro Obata

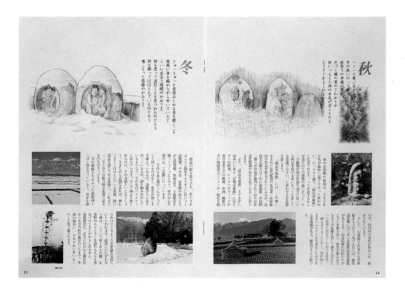

1. 穂高町観光協会 Hotaka Town Tourist Association　パンフレット　Pamphlet　1994　DF: ヨシダ印刷 Yoshida Printing

2. 大和町 Yamato Town　パンフレット　Pamphlet　1994　CD, CW: 高橋修宏 Nobuhiro Takahashi　AD, D: 滝川正弘 Masahiro Takigawa　P: 金子徳彦 Norihiko Kaneko/福田光祐 Mitsuhiro Fukuda/etc　DF: ㈲クロス Cross, Inc.

1. 東由利町役場 Higashiyuri Town パンフレット Pamphlet

2. 石巻市 Ishimaki City パンフレット Pamphlet 1994

1, 2, 4. 和歌山県 Wakayama Prefecture　ポスター　Posters 1994　CD: 岡田和也 Kazuya Okada　AD, D: 田中裕也 Hiroya Tanaka　D: 春名 勝 Masaru Haruna　P: 富浦隆則 Takanori Tomiura　CW: 佐々木繁和 Shigekazu Sasaki
DF: 田中裕也デザイン事務所 Tanaka Hiroya Design Office　A: 博報堂 Hakuhodo Incorporated

3. 三朝町役場 Misasa Town　ポスター　Poster 1994　AD, D, CW: 井上八重美 Yaemi Inoue　P: 川田 宏 Hiroshi Kawata　DF: ㈲アイ・カンパニー I. Company Inc.

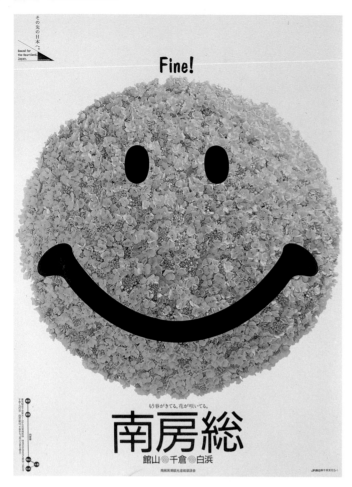

1. 南房黒潮観光連絡協議会 Nanbo Kuroshio Tourist Association ポスター Poster 1993 CD, CW: 川名融郎 Michiro Kawana AD, D: 永井栄子 Eiko Nagai P: 宮川幹夫 Mikio Miyagawa DF: ㈱コア Core Corporation

2. 丸山町 Maruyama Town ポスター Poster 1993 CD, AD: 川名融郎 Michiro Kawana D: 永井栄子 Eiko Nagai P: 宮川幹夫 Mikio Miyagawa CW: 家城大樹 Daiki Yashiro DF: ㈱コア Core Corporation

3. ギリシア政府観光局 Greek National Tourist Organization ポスター Poster 1994 CD: 関橋英作 Eisaku Sekihashi AD: 松永ひさ Hisa Matsunaga D: 久江康裕 Yasuhiro Hisae P: 出戸規善 Kizen Deto CW: 結城喜宣 Yoshinobu Yuki
   DF: ㈱グリップ Grip, Inc. Typographer: 築紫 Tsukushi A: ウォルタートンプソンジャパン㈱ J. Walter Thompson Japan Limited

4. ギリシア政府観光局 Greek National Tourist Organization ポスター Poster 1994 CD: 関橋英作 Eisaku Sekihashi AD: 松永ひさ Hisa Matsunaga D: 久江康裕 Yasuhiro Hisae P: 熊倉俊哉 Toshiya Kumakura CW: 結城喜宣 Yoshinobu Yuki
   DF: ㈱グリップ Grip, Inc. Typographer: 築紫 Tsukushi A: ウォルタートンプソンジャパン㈱ J. Walter Thompson Japan Limited

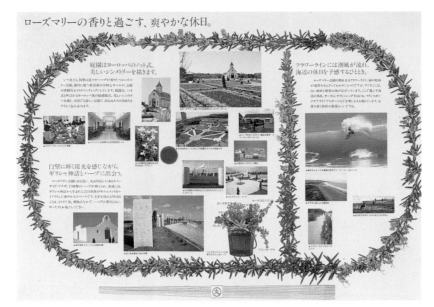

1. 丸山町 Maruyama Town　パンフレット　Pamphlet 1993 CD, AD: 川名融郎 Michiro Kawana D: 永井栄子 Eiko Nagai P: 宮川幹夫 Mikio Miyagawa CW: 家城大樹 Daiki Yashiro DF: ㈱コア Core Corporation

2. 丸山町振興公社 Maruyama Public Corporation　リーフレット　Leaflets 1992-94 CD, CW, P: 川名融郎 Michiro Kawana AD, D: 永井栄子 Eiko Nagai DF: ㈱コア Core Corporation

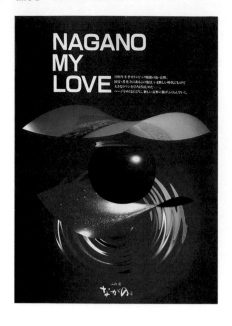

1. 長野市商工部観光課 Nagano City Tourist Bureau　パンフレット　Pamphlet 1992 CD: 中村 彩 Aya Nakamura　D: 北沢映男 Teruo Kitazawa　CW: 川崎史郎 Shiro Kawasaki

2. 清音村役場 Kiyone Village　パンフレット　Pamphlet 1994 DF: コーホク商事㈲ Kohoku Shoji

1. 大野市役所商工観光課 Ono City パンフレット Pamphlet 1989 DF: エーアンドエス A&S

2. 名古屋観光コンベンションビューロー Nagoya Convention & Visitors Bureau パンフレット Pamphlet 1993 CD: 磯谷秀史 Hideshi Isogai D: 中北直子 Naoko Nakakita P: 佐宗 剛 Tsuyoshi Saso CW: 伊藤まゆみ Mayumi Ito
DF: インノースデザインオフィース Innosu Design Office/東洋地図 Toyo Map Company Limited Map: 羽柴良三 Ryozo Hashiba

■　TRANSPORTATION SERVICES　交通機関　■

1, 2, 3, 5. 東日本旅客鉄道 East Japan Railway 旅客鉄道会社/ポスター Rail company/Posters CD: 大島征夫 Yukio Oshima AD: 金森周一 Shuichi Kanamori D: 座間 薫 Kaoru Zama P: 藤井 保 Tamotsu Fujii CW: 秋山 晶 Sho Akiyama
PD: 小林 明 Akira Kobayashi I: 横山 明 Akira Yokoyama DF: ライトパブリシティ Light Publicity Ltd./金森広告事務所 Kanamori Advertising Office A: JR東日本企画 East Japan Marketing & Communications, Inc./電通 Dentsu, Inc.

4, 6. 東日本旅客鉄道 East Japan Railway 旅客鉄道会社/ポスター Rail company/Posters CD: 大島征夫 Yukio Oshima AD: 金森周一 Shuichi Kanamori D: 座間 薫 Kaoru Zama I: 横山 明 Akira Yokoyama P: 宮永慶太 Keita Miyanaga
CW: 秋山 晶 Sho Akiyama PD: 小林 明 Akira Kobayashi DF: ライトパブリシティ Light Publicity Ltd./金森広告事務所 Kanamori Advertising Office A: JR東日本企画 East Japan Marketing & Communications, Inc./電通 Dentsu, Inc.

1. 東日本旅客鉄道 East Japan Railway 旅客鉄道会社／ポスター Rail company/Poster CD: 大島征夫 Yukio Oshima AD: 金森周一 Shuichi Kanamori D: 座間 薫 Kaoru Zama P: 小林 鷹 Taka Kobayashi CW: 秋山 晶 Sho Akiyama
PD: 小林 明 Akira Kobayashi DF: ライトパブリシティ Light Publicity Ltd.／金森広告事務所 Kanamori Advertising Office A: JR東日本企画 East Japan Marketing & Communications, Inc.／電通 Dentsu, Inc.

2, 3. 東日本旅客鉄道 East Japan Railway 旅客鉄道会社／ポスター Rail company/Posters CD: 大島征夫 Yukio Oshima AD: 金森周一 Shuichi Kanamori D: 座間 薫 Kaoru Zama P: 木津康夫 Yasuo Kizu CW: 秋山 晶 Sho Akiyama
PD: 小林 明 Akira Kobayashi DF: ライトパブリシティ Light Publicity Ltd.／金森広告事務所 Kanamori Advertising Office A: JR東日本企画 East Japan Marketing & Communications, Inc.／電通 Dentsu, Inc.

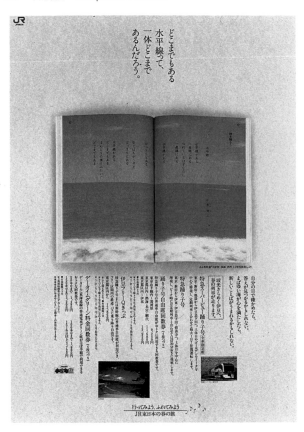

どこまでもある
水平線って、
一体どこまで
あるんだろう。

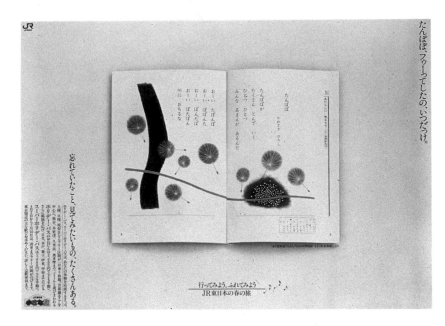

たんぽぽ、フゥーってしたの、いつだっけ。

行ってみよう、ふれてみよう
JR東日本の春の旅

セーターにくっつく草、いくつ知ってる？

自分の足で歩いたら、わかるかもしれない。

行ってみよう、ふれてみよう
JR東日本の春の旅

出かけたら、
ずっとじょうずに
歌えた。

行ってみよう、ふれてみよう
JR東日本の春の旅

東日本旅客鉄道 East Japan Railway 旅客鉄道会社／ポスター Rail company/Posters 1994 CD: 福井 寛 Hiroshi Fukui AD: 内山保治 Yasuji Uchiyama D: 川上康一 Koichi Kawakami P: ㈱エフエイト F8 CW: 鈴木良平 Ryohei Suzuki DF: ㈱ケイエヌプランニング KN Planning, Inc.

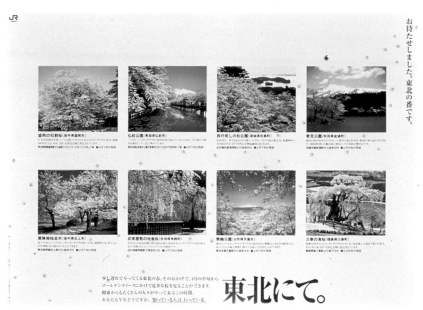

1, 2. **東日本旅客鉄道 East Japan Railway** 旅客鉄道会社/ポスター　Rail company/Posters　1995　CD: 福井 寛 Hiroshi Fukui　AD: 内山保治 Yasuji Uchiyama　D: 国吉 勝 Masaru Kuniyoshi　CW: 白石大介 Daisuke Shiraishi
　　DF: ㈱ケイエヌプランニング KN Planning, Inc.

3. **東日本旅客鉄道 East Japan Railway** 旅客鉄道会社/ポスター　Rail company/Poster　1995　CD: 福井 寛 Hiroshi Fukui　AD: 内山保治 Yasuji Uchiyama　D: 川上康一 Koichi Kawakami　P: 伊吹 徹 Toru Ibuki
　　CW: 白石大介 Daisuke Shiraishi　DF: ㈱ケイエヌプランニング KN Planning, Inc.

東日本旅客鉄道 East Japan Railway　旅客鉄道会社/ポスター　Railway company/Posters CD, CW: 武藤庄ハ S. Muto AD: 村中恒彦 T. Muranaka D: 小島健児 K. Kojima P: 福永代志時 Y. Fukunaga CW: 後藤健太郎 Kentaro Goto
DF: ライブ・アネックス Live Annex

1
2
3
4
5
6

1. 東武鉄道 Tobu Tetsudo　鉄道会社/ポスター　Rail company/Poster　CD, D: 深見 晃 Akira Fukami　P: 大久保和夫 Kazuo Okubo　CW: 平田夏樹 Natsuki Hirata　2. 東日本旅客鉄道 East Japan Railway　旅客鉄道会社/パンフレット
Rail company/Pamphlet　1994　CD: 福井 寛 Hiroshi Fukui　AD: 内山保治 Yasuji Uchiyama　D: 川上康一 Koichi Kawakami　P: 吉岡清彦 Kiyohiko Yoshioka　CW: 高橋 朗 Akira Takahashi　DF: ㈱ケイエヌプランニング KN Planning, Inc.
3. 東日本旅客鉄道 East Japan Railway　旅客鉄道会社/ポスター　Rail company/Poster　1994　CD: 福井 寛 Hiroshi Fukui　AD: 内山保治 Yasuji Uchiyama　D: 川上康一 Koichi Kawakami　P: 真島満秀写真事務所 Majima Mitsuhide Photo Office
CW: 白石大介 Daisuke Shiraishi　DF: ㈱ケイエヌプランニング KN Planning, Inc.　4. 東日本旅客鉄道 East Japan Railway　旅客鉄道会社/パンフレット　Rail company/Pamphlet　1994　CD: 福井 寛 Hiroshi Fukui
AD: 内山保治 Yasuji Uchiyama　D: 川上康一 Koichi Kawakami　P: 真島満秀写真事務所 Majima Mitsuhide Photo Office　CW: 白石大介 Daisuke Shiraishi/高橋 朗 Akira Takahashi　DF: ㈱ケイエヌプランニング KN Planning, Inc.
5, 6. 東日本旅客鉄道 East Japan Railway　旅客鉄道会社/ポスター　Rail company/Posters　CD, CW: 武藤庄八 S. Muto　AD: 村中恒彦 Tsunehiko Muranaka　D: 小島健児 K. Kojima　P: 福永代志時 Y. Fukunaga　CW: 後藤健太郎 Kentaro Goto
DF: ライブ・アネックス Live Annex

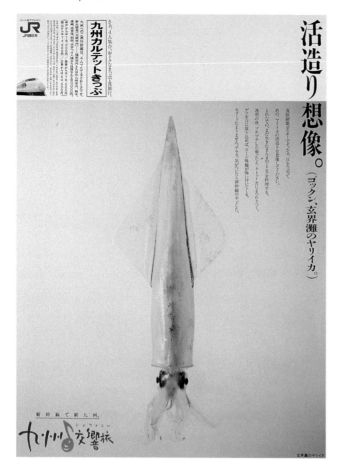

JR西日本 West Japan Railways 旅客鉄道会社/ポスター Rail company/Posters CD: 井上光央 Mitsuo Inoue AD: 藤井宏徳 Hironori Fujii AD, D: 田中元信 Motonobu Tanaka D: 田島康寛 Yasuhiro Tajima P: 山下一夫 Kazuo Yamashita
CW: 田中有史 Yuji Tanaka DF: ㈱マック MAQ Inc.

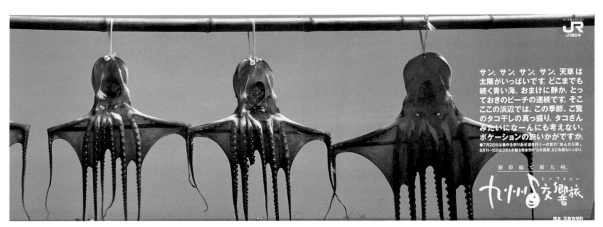

1. **JR西日本 West Japan Railways** 旅客鉄道会社／ポスター　Rail company/Posters CD: 井上光央 Mitsuo Inoue AD: 藤井宏徳 Hironori Fujii AD, D: 田中元信 Motonobu Tanaka D: 中井延年 Nobutoshi Nakai P: 山下一夫 Kazuo Yamashita
CW: 田中有史 Yuji Tanaka DF: ㈱マック MAQ Inc.

2. **JR西日本 West Japan Railways** 旅客鉄道会社／ポスター　Rail company/Posters CD: 井上光央 Mitsuo Inoue AD: 藤井宏徳 Hironori Fujii AD, D: 田中元信 Motonobu Tanaka P: 山下一夫 Kazuo Yamashita CW: 田中有史 Yuji Tanaka
DF: ㈱マック MAQ Inc.

1, 2. JRグループ **JR Group** 旅客鉄道会社/アナウンスメント Rail company/Announcements CD: 大島征夫 Yukio Oshima AD: 込山富秀 Tomihide Komiyama/畑野憲一 Kenichi Hatano D: 大高 泉 Izumi Otaka P: 恩田義則 Yoshinori Onda
CW: 佐藤澄子 Sumiko Sato/山田紀子 Noriko Yamada

3. JR東日本千葉支社 **East Japan Railways** 旅客鉄道会社/ポスター Rail company/Poster 1991 CD, AD: 郡司由夫 Yoshio Gunji D: 川口久美子 Kumiko Kawaguchi P: 大坪智秋 Chiaki Otsubo DF: ㈱G2 G2 Co., Ltd.

1, 2. **JR西日本 West Japan Railways** 旅客鉄道会社／ポスター　Rail company/Posters　CD: 井上光央 Mitsuo Inoue　AD: 藤井宏徳 Hironori Fujii　AD, D: 田中元信 Motonobu Tanaka　D: 中井延年 Nobutoshi Nakai　P: 山下一夫 Kazuo Yamashita
　　CW: 粟野広子 Hiroko Awano／多田伸一 Shinichi Tada　DF: ㈱マック MAQ Inc.

3. **JR西日本 West Japan Railways** 旅客鉄道会社／ポスター　Rail company/Poster　CD: 井上光央 Mitsuo Inoue　AD: 藤井宏徳 Hironori Fujii　AD, D: 田中元信 Motonobu Tanaka　D: 苧田健一 Kenichi Odo　P: 山下一夫 Kazuo Yamashita
　　CW: 田中有史 Yuji Tanaka　DF: ㈱マック MAQ Inc.

4. **はとバス Hato Bus** バス会社／パンフレット　Bus company/Pamphlet 1995　I: 加藤裕将 Hiromasa Kato

1, 2. 福井県 Fukui Prefecture　ポスター Posters 1993 CD: 酒井晶司 Seiji Sakai　AD: 佐野元彦 Motohiko Sano　D: 種茂幸也 Yukiya Tanemo　I: 加藤順也 Junya Kato　CW: 小澤 聡 Satoshi Ozawa　DF: ㈱キューズデザイン Quiz Co., Ltd.

3. JR九州 Kyushu Railways　旅客鉄道会社/情報誌 Rail company/Information pamphlets 1995 CD, AD: 藤原政彦 Masahiko Fujiwara　D, I, DF: シー・ディー・ビー C・D・B　P: 水本勝美 Katsumi Mizumoto　CW: 木下智恵子 Chieko Kinoshita

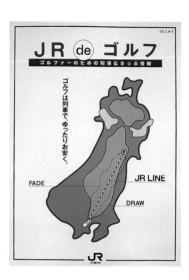

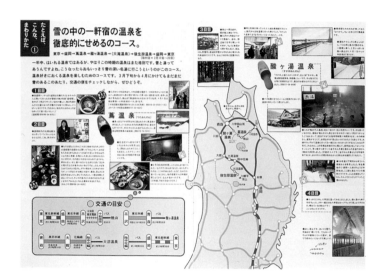

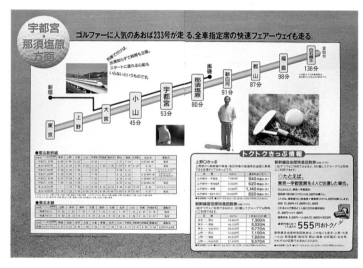

1. 東日本旅客鉄道 East Japan Railway 旅客鉄道会社/パンフレット Rail company/Pamphlet 1995 CD: 福井 寛 Hiroshi Fukui AD: 内山保治 Yasuji Uchiyama D: 川上康一 Koichi Kawakami P: 伊吹 徹 Toru Ibuki
CW: 白石大介 Daisuke Shiraishi DF: ㈱ケイエヌプランニング KN Planning, Inc.

2. 東日本旅客鉄道 East Japan Railway 旅客鉄道会社/パンフレット Rail company/Pamphlet 1995 CD: 福井 寛 Hiroshi Fukui AD: 内山保治 Yasuji Uchiyama D: 川上康一 Koichi Kawakami CW: 高橋 朗 Akira Takahashi
DF: ㈱ケイエヌプランニング KN Planning, Inc.

1. **東武鉄道 Tobu Tetsudo** 旅客鉄道会社／ポスター　Rail company/Poster 1992 CD: 深見 晃 Akira Fukami AD: 財津昌樹 Masaki Zaitsu D: 船水正和 Masakazu Funamizu P: 大久保和夫 Kazuo Okubo CW: 小松圭一 Keiichi Komatsu

2, 3, 4. **東武鉄道 Tobu Tetsudo** 旅客鉄道会社／ポスター　Rail company/Posters 1992-93 CD, D: 深見 晃 Akira Fukami P: 大久保和夫 Kazuo Okubo CW: 横田明子 Akiko Yokota

5, 6. **野岩鉄道 Yagan Tetsudo** 旅客鉄道会社／ポスター　Rail company/Posters 1993 CD, D: 深見 晃 Akira Fukami P: 大久保和夫 Kazuo Okubo I: 橘田幸雄 Sachio Kitsuta CW: 横田明子 Akiko Yokota

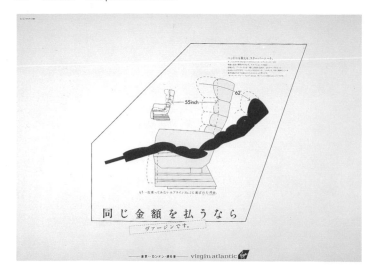

ヴァージンアトランティック航空 Virgin Atlantic Airways 航空会社/ポスター Airline/Posters CD, AD: 金森周一 Shuichi Kanamori D: 座間 薫 Kaoru Zama P: 内藤忠行 Tadayuki Naito CW: 梅本洋一 Yoichi Umemoto
PD: 柳澤剛雄 Takao Yanagisawa

■　　LEISURE FACILITIES　　レジャー施設　　■

1, 2. 北蔵王笹谷開発、セントメリー Kitazao Sasaya Kaihatsu, St. Mary　スキー場/ポスター　Ski resort/Posters　CD: 鈴木隆則 Takanori Suzuki　AD, D: 北里典明 Noriaki Kitazato　D: 遠藤菊香 Kikuka Endo　CW: 猪股 司 Tsukasa Inomata
　　P: 只野浩樹 Hiroki Tadano　Artwork: 龍高社 Ryukosha

3. 北蔵王笹谷開発、セントメリー Kitazao Sasaya Kaihatsu, St. Mary　スキー場/ポスター　Ski resort/Poster　CD: 鈴木隆則 Takanori Suzuki　AD, D: 北里典明 Noriaki Kitazato　CW: 猪股 司 Tsukasa Inomata　P: 金子正明 Masaaki Kaneko

4. 北蔵王笹谷開発、セントメリー Kitazao Sasaya Kaihatsu, St. Mary　スキー場/ポスター　Ski resort/Poster　CD: 鈴木隆則 Takanori Suzuki　AD: 北里典明 Noriaki Kitazato　D: 遠藤菊香 Kikuka Endo　CW: 猪股 司 Tsukasa Inomata
　　P: 梅原 章 Akira Umehara

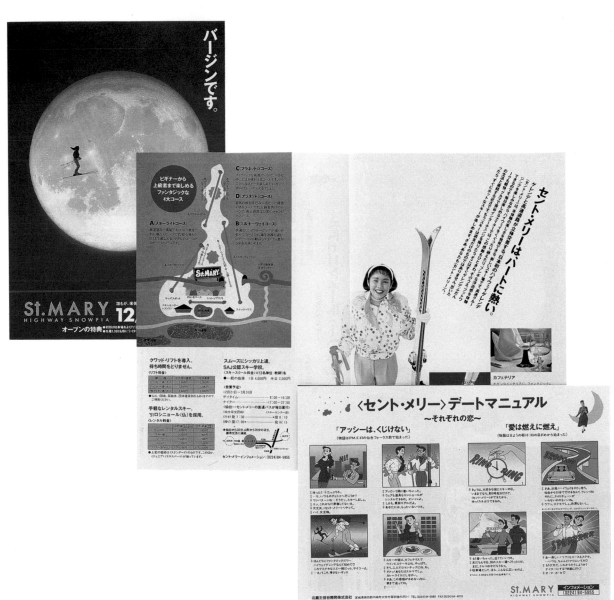

1. 北蔵王笹谷開発．セントメリー Kitazao Sasaya Kaihatsu, St. Mary　スキー場/パンフレット　Ski resort/Pamphlet　CD: 鈴木隆則 Takanori Suzuki　AD, D: 北里典明 Noriaki Kitazato　D: 遠藤菊香 Kikuka Endo　CW: 猪股 司 Tsukasa Inomata
　P: 只野浩樹 Hiroki Tadano　Artwork: 龍高社 Ryukosha
2. 北蔵王笹谷開発．セントメリー Kitazao Sasaya Kaihatsu, St. Mary　スキー場/各種案内　Ski resort/Announcements　CD: 鈴木隆則 Takanori Suzuki　AD, D: 北里典明 Noriaki Kitazato　CW: 猪股 司 Tsukasa Inomata　P: 金子正明 Masaaki Kaneko

1, 2. 東京サマーランド Tokyo Summer Land　レジャーランド/ポスター　Amusement park/Posters　1990　CD, CW: 高山宗晴（東急エージェンシー）Muneharu Takayama　AD: 渡辺克巳 Katsumi Watanabe　D: 千葉 毅 Takeshi Chiba
　　P: 芝田満之 Mitsuyuki Shibata　DF: ㈱アドフォックス Adfox Co., Ltd.

3, 4, 5, 6. 東京サマーランド Tokyo Summer Land　レジャーランド/ポスター　Amusement park/Posters　1991　CD, CW: 高山宗晴（東急エージェンシー）Muneharu Takayama　AD: 渡辺克巳 Katsumi Watanabe　D: 千葉 毅 Takeshi Chiba
　　P: 鶴田直樹 Naoki Tsuruta　DF: ㈱アドフォックス Adfox Co., Ltd.

東京サマーランド Tokyo Summer Land レジャーランド/ポスター Amusement park/Posters 1992 CD, CW: 高山宗晴（東急エージェンシー）Muneharu Takayama AD: 渡辺克巳 Katsumi Watanabe D: 坂井栄一 Eiichi Sakai/
小佐治和幸 Kazuyuki Kosaji P: 相川喜伸 Yoshinobu Aikawa DF: ㈱アドフォックス Adfox Co., Ltd.

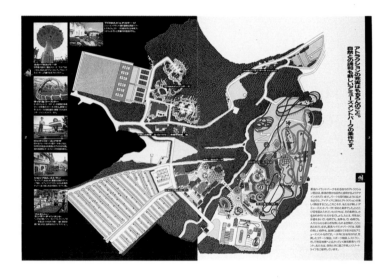

藤和那須リゾート、那須ハイランドパーク Nasu Highland Park　レジャーランド/パンフレット　Amusement park/Pamphlets　1992　CD: 小松 誠 Makoto Komatsu　AD, D: 細山田光宣 Mitsunobu Hosoyamada　P: 貝塚純一 Junichi Kaizuka
I: 大村公一郎 Koichiro Omura　CW: 西田善太 Zenta Nishida　DF: ㈱細山田デザイン事務所 Hosoyamada Design Office

1. High Wind Center Margarita　ウィンドサーフィン・リゾート/パンフレット　Windsurfing resort/Pamphlet　1993　CD, AD, D, P, I: Greg Stevenson　DF: Toast

2. 小田急電鉄, ファミリーランド Odakyu Electric Railway　遊園地/チラシ　Amusement park/Flyer　CD: 中山 寿 Hisashi Nakayama　AD, D: 山本隆一 Ryuichi Yamamoto　P: 写楽苦 Sharaku　I: 大久保敏邦 Toshikuni Okubo/ジップス Zips
CW: 加藤良夫 Yoshio Kato/吉田英司 Eiji Yoshida

1. ワイルドブルーヨコハマ Wild Blue Yokohama プール/チラシ Pool/Flyer

2, 4. 京急開発 Keikyu Kaihatsu スキー場/ポスター Ski resort/Posters 1994 CD: 門屋 奏 Tai Kadoya AD, D, CW: 飯塚兼悟 Kengo Iizuka P: 菊地正人 Masato Kikuchi CW: 陣上栄里 Eri Jingami DF: エヌ・エイ・ダヴリュ N.A.W.
A: 京急アドエンタープライズ Keikyu Ad Enterprise

3. 小田急電鉄 Odakyu Electric Railway プール/ポスター Pool/Poster 1994 AD: 市川清崇 Kiyotaka Ichikawa D: 金子裕美 Hiromi Kaneko CW: 関かおり Kaori Seki DF: 南青山事務所 Minami Aoyama Jimusho Co., Ltd.

1. 小田急電鉄 **Odakyu Electric Railway** レジャーランド／ポスター　Amusement park/Poster　CD, AD: 荒井耕治 Koji Arai　D: 鈴木英樹 Hideki Suzuki　P: 山田 覚 Satoru Yamada　CW: 坂田元玄 Motoharu Sakata
　　DF: ㈱タイム T. I. M. E. Co., Ltd./㈲アライ事務所 Arai Office Inc.

2. 小田急電鉄 **Odakyu Electric Railway** レジャーランド／ポスター　Amusement park/Poster　CD, AD: 荒井耕治 Koji Arai　D: 鈴木英樹 Hideki Suzuki　I: 田中靖夫 Yasuo Tanaka　CW: 坂田元玄 Motoharu Sakata
　　DF: ㈱タイム T. I. M. E. Co., Ltd./㈲アライ事務所 Arai Office Inc.

3. 小田急電鉄 **Odakyu Electric Railway** レジャーランド／ポスター　Amusement park/Poster　CD, AD: 荒井耕治 Koji Arai　D: 鈴木英樹 Hideki Suzuki　P: 中野博司 Hiroshi Nakano　CW: 阿相久美子 Kumiko Aso
　　DF: ㈱タイム T. I. M. E. Co., Ltd./㈲アライ事務所 Arai Office Inc.

4. 富士急ハイランド **Fujikyu High-Land** レジャーランド／ポスター　Amusement park/Poster 1995 CD: 大蔵良章 Joe Okura/進藤 智 Satoshi Shindo AD, D: 高木慶一 Keiichi Takagi
　　P: コスモ＆アクション＋クラフトワーク Cosmo & Action, Craftwork　CW: 朝生謙二 Kenji Asao　DF: 高木慶一デザイン室 Keiichi Takagi Design Room

1, 2. 白馬観光開発 Hakuba Kanko Kaihatsu スキー場/ポスター Ski resort/Posters 1990-91 CD: 竹内 寛 Kan Takeuchi CD, AD: 稲島 慎 Shin Inajima D: 岩瀬 真 Makoto Iwase/小林 武 Tukeshi Kobayashi P: 鈴木恒彦 Isunehiko Suzuki
CW: 中居泰雅 Yasumasa Nakai DF: ㈱ジャストアドメイク Just Ad Make Co., Ltd.

3. 会津高原観光開発 Aizukogen Kankokaihatsu スキー場/パンフレット Ski resort/Pamphlet 1992 CD, AD: 石川三郎 Saburo Ishikawa D: 高谷 一 Hajime Takaya P: 佐藤 淳 Jun Sato CW: 鈴木博信 Hironobu Suzuki
DF: ㈱リンクスアドバタイジング Links Advertising Inc.

4. ホテルグリーンプラザ白馬, 白馬コルチナ国際スキー場 Hotel Green Plaza Hakuba, Hakuba Cortina Kokusai ホテル、スキー場/ポスター Hotel & Ski resort/Poster 1993 CD, CW: 近藤克己 Katsumi Kondo AD: 後藤雄一 Yuichi Goto
D: 大日方陽子 Yoko Obinata P: 富山 修 Osamu Toyama DF: ㈱グリップ Grip, Inc. A: 中央宣興㈱ Chuosenko Advertising Co., Ltd.

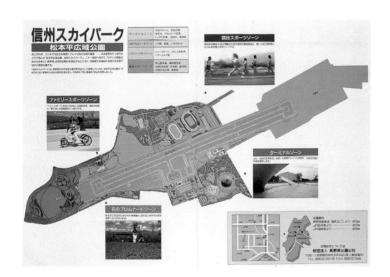

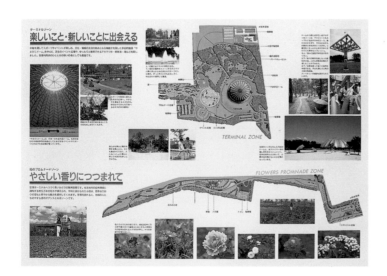

1. 長野県公園公社、信州スカイパーク Shinshu Sky Park 公園/パンフレット Park/Pamphlet 1994 CD, AD, D: 麻生克之 Katsuyuki Aso P: 柳沢寛幸 Hiroyuki Yanagisawa I: イデア ファクトリー Idea Factory CW: 麻生光子 Mitsuko Aso

2. 長野県公園公社、やまびこドーム Yamabiko Dome パンフレット Pamphlet 1994 CD, AD, D: 麻生克之 Katsuyuki Aso P: 柳沢寛幸 Hiroyuki Yanagisawa I: 田中 孝 Takashi Tanaka CW: 麻生光子 Mitsuko Aso

MUJI Outdoor Network

自然となかよくなれる場所。
無印良品のキャンプ場。

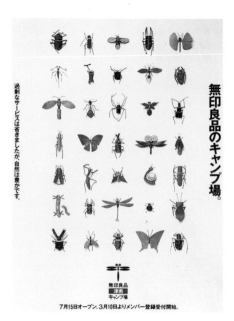

7月15日オープン。3月10日よりメンバー登録受付開始。

1, 2. 良品計画 Ryohin Keikaku　キャンプ場/リーフレット、チラシ　Camping facility/leaflet, Flyer

3. 大阪府、クイーンズランド庭園 Osaka Prefecture, Queens Land Garden　公園/施設案内パンフレット　Public garden/Facilities pamphlet　CD, AD, D: 植 章修 Akinobu Ue　CW: 藤田 文 Fumi Fujita

東京動物園協会 Tokyo Zoological Park Society 動物園/パンフレット Zoo/Pamphlet 1993 CD: 境 修一郎 Shuichiro Sakai AD: 前原由紀夫 Yukio Maehara D: 松井貴子 Takako Matsui
P, CW: (財)東京動物園協会 Tokyo Zoological Park DF: ㈱ボーダー Border Inc.

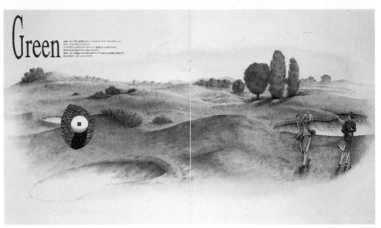

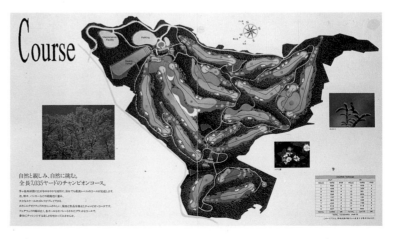

ダイワレジャーリゾート Daiwa Leisure Resort　ゴルフ場/会員募集パンフレット　Golf course/Membership promotion pamphlet　1991　CD: 上原正光 Masamitsu Uehara　AD, D: 坂田直樹 Naoki Sakata　P: 佐藤 淳 Jun Sato
I: 金 斗鉉 Kim Tougen/永田信行 Nobuyuki Nagata　CW: 伊藤英姿 Eishi Ito　DF: ㈱スタジオゲット Studio Get Co., Ltd.

名門にふさわしい豊潤の時。
心からくつろげるクラブライフを。

TIGERS GOLF CLUB

タイガースゴルフクラブ

巧妙にレイアウトされ、
プレーヤーのチャレンジ意欲をかきたてる18のコース。

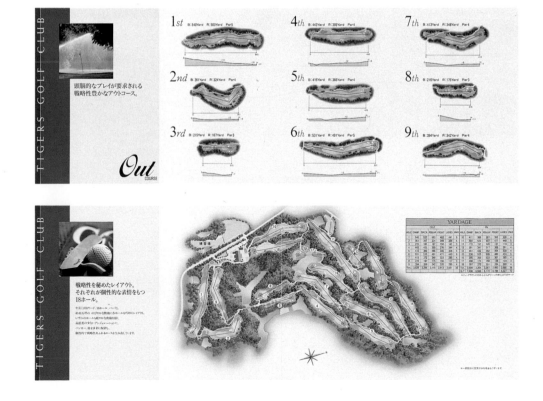

TIGERS GOLF CLUB

Out COURSE

頭脳的なプレイが要求される
戦略性豊かなアウトコース。

戦略性を秘めたレイアウト。
それぞれが個性的な表情をもつ
18ホール。

阪神総合レジャー　ゴルフ場/会員募集パンフレット　Golf course/Membership promotion pamphlet　1991　AD: 高野眞逸六 Shinichiro Takano　D: 川崎 S. Kawasaki／井上 J. Inoue　CW: 藤井 M.Fujii
DF: トーワクリエイティブ㈱ Towa Creative Inc.　A: ㈱大広 Daiko

1. 北海道緑化開発 Hokkaido Ryokkakaihatsu　ゴルフ場/総合案内パンフレット　Golf course/General information pamphlet 1991 CD, AD, CW: 堤 啓隆 Hirotaka Tsutsumi D: 工藤真由美 Mayumi Kudoh P: ブライアン モーガン Brian Morgan
　DF: オーガン Organ Co.

2. 新星開発 Shinsei Development　ゴルフ場/情報誌　Golf course/Information pamphlets 1994 CD: 安居和弘 Kazuhiro Yasui AD, D: 菅野昭一 Shoichi Sugano P: 大東照男 Teruo Daito/山下隆司 Takashi Yamashita I: 永野敬子 Keiko Nagano
　CW: 滝本信子 Nobuko Takimoto DF: ㈱チャンスオペレーション Chance Operation

■　　SUBMITTORS' INDEX　　作品提供者索引　　■

海外作品　Overseas

Travel & Leisure Graphics

ART DIRECTOR
Miyuki Kawanabe

EDITOR
Yuko Yoshio

BUSINESS MANAGER
Masato Ieshiro

PHOTOGRAPHER
Kuniharu Fujimoto

ENGLISH TRANSLATOR AND CONSULTANT
Sue Herbert

PUBLISHER
Shingo Miyoshi

1995年10月16日初版第1刷発行

定価 16,000 円 （本体15,534円）

発行所　ピエ・ブックス
〒170　東京都豊島区駒込4-14-6-301
TEL: 03-3949-5010 FAX: 03-3949-5650

印刷・製本　エバーベストプリンティング ㈱
Printed and bound by Everbest Printing Co., Ltd.

Ko Fai Industrial Building, Block C5, 10th Floor
7 Ko Fai Road, Yau Tong, Kowloon, Hong Kong
Tel: 852-2727-4433 Fax: 852-2772-7908

ISBN 4-938586-87-8 C3070 P16000E

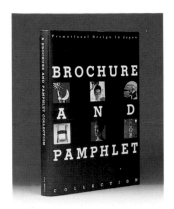

BROCHURE & PAMPHLET COLLECTION 1
Pages: 224(144 in color) ¥15,000
業種別カタログ・コレクション
Here are hundreds of the best brochures and pamphlets from Japan.
This collection will make a valuable sourcebook for anyone involved in corporate identity advertising and graphic design.

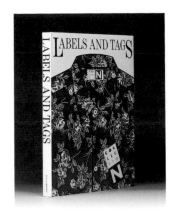

LABELS AND TAGS
Pages: 224(192 in color) ¥15,000
ファッションのラベル&タグ・コレクション
Over 1,600 garment labels representing 450 brands produced in Japan are included in this full-color collection.

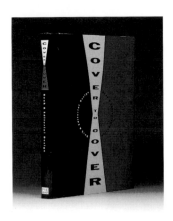

COVER TO COVER
Pages: 240(176 in color) ¥17,000
世界のブック&エディトリアル・デザイン
The latest trends in book and magazine design are illustrated with over 1,000 creative works by international firms.

BUSINESS STATIONERY GRAPHICS 1
Pages: 224(192 in color) ¥15,000
世界のレターヘッド・コレクション
Creatively designed letterheads, business cards, memo pads, and other business forms and documents are included this international collection.

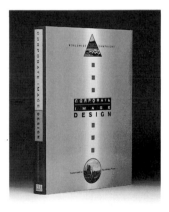

CORPORATE IMAGE DESIGN
Pages: 336(272 in color) ¥16,000
世界の業種別CI・ロゴマーク
This collection presents the best corporate identity projects from around the world. Creative and effective designs from top international firms are featured in this valuable source book.

POSTCARD GRAPHICS 3
Pages: 232(208 in color) ¥16,000
世界の業種別ポストカード・コレクション
Volume 3 in the series presents more than 1,200 promotional postcards in dazzling full color. Top designers from the world over have contributed to this useful image bank of ideas.

GRAPHIC BEAT London / Tokyo 1 & 2
Pages: 224(208 in color) ¥16,000
音楽とグラフィックのコラボレーション
1,500 music-related graphic works from 29 of the hottest designers in Tokyo and London. Features Malcolm Garrett, Russell Miles, Tadanori Yokoo, Neville Brody, Vaughn Oliver and others.

BUSINESS CARD GRAPHICS 2
Pages: 224(192 In color) ¥16,000
世界の名刺&ショップカード、第2弾
This latest collection presents 1,000 creative cards from international designers. Features hundreds of cards used in creative fields such as graphic design and architecture.

T-SHIRT GRAPHICS
Pages: 224(192 in color) ¥16,000
世界のTシャツ・グラフィックス
This unique collection showcases 700 wonderfully creative T-Shirt designs from the world's premier design centers. Grouped according to theme, categories include sports, casual, designer and promotional shirts among others.

DIAGRAM GRAPHICS
Pages: 224(192 in color) ¥16,000
世界のダイアグラム・デザインの集大成
Hundreds of unique and lucid diagrams, charts, graphs, maps and technical illustrations from leading international design firms. Variety of media represented including computer graphics.

SPECIAL EVENT GRAPHICS
Pages: 224(192 in color) ¥16,000
世界のイベント・グラフィックス特集
This innovative collection features design elements from concerts, festivals, fashion shows, symposiums and more. International works include posters, tickets, flyers, invitations and various premiers.

RETAIL IDENTITY GRAPHICS
Pages: 208(176 in color) ¥14,800
世界のショップ・グラフィックス
This visually exciting collection showcases the identity design campaigns of restaurants, bars, shops and various other retailers. Wide variety of pieces are featured including business cards, signs, menus, bags and hundreds more.

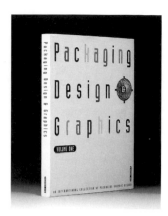

PACKAGING DESIGN & GRAPHICS 1
Pages: 224(192 in color) ¥16,000
世界の業種別パッケージ・デザイン
An international collection featuring 400 creative and exciting package designs from renowned designers.

ADVERTISING GREETING CARDS 3
Pages: 224(176 in color) ¥16,000
世界のダイレクトメール集大成、第3弾
The best-selling series continues with this collection of elegantly designed advertising pieces from a wide variety of categories. This exciting image bank of ideas will interest all graphic designers and direct mail specialists.

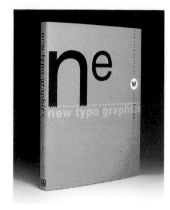

NEW TYPO GRAPHICS
Pages: 224(192 in color) ¥16,000
世界の最新タイポグラフィ・コレクション
New and innovative typographical works gathered from top designers around the world. A wide variety of type applications are shown including posters, brochures, CD jackets, calendars, book designs and more.

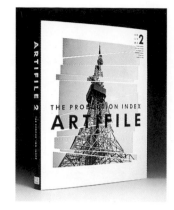

The Production Index ARTIFILE 2
Pages: 244(240 in color) ¥13,500
活躍中！最新プロダクション年鑑、第2弾
A design showcase featuring the best works from 115 graphic design studios, photographers, and creators in Japan. Works shown include print advertisements, corporate identity pieces, commercial photography and illustration.

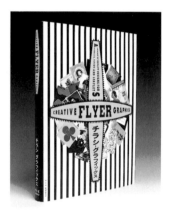

CREATIVE FLYER GRAPHICS
Pages: 224(176 in color) ¥16,000
チラシ・グラフィックス
Features about 500 rigorously screened flyers and leaflets. You see what superior graphics can accomplish on a single sheet of paper. This is an invaluable reference to all your advertising production for years to come.

1, 2 & 3 COLOR GRAPHICS
Pages: 208(Full Color) ¥16,000
1・2・3色 グラフィックス
See about 300 samples of 1, 2 & 3 color artwork that are so expressive they often surpass the impact of full 4 color reproductions. This is a very important book that will expand the possibilities of your design works in the future.

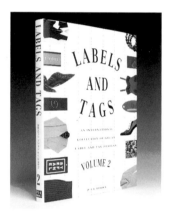

LABELS AND TAGS 2
Pages: 224(192 in color) ¥16,000
世界のラベル＆タグ・コレクション　2
This long-awaited second volume features 1500 samples representing 400 top name-brands from around the world.

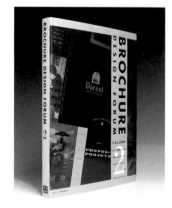

BROCHURE DESIGN FORUM 2
Pages: 224(176 in color) ¥16,000
世界の最新カタログ・コレクション　2
Features 70 businesses and 250 reproductions for a complete overview of the latest and best in brochure design.

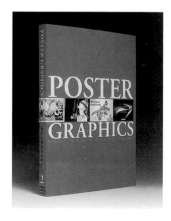

POSTER GRAPHICS 2
Pages: 256(192 in color) ¥17,000
業種別世界のポスター集大成
700 posters from the top creators in Japan and abroad are showcased in this book - classified by business. This invaluable reference makes it easy to compare design trends among various industries and corporations.

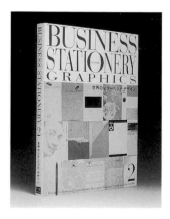

BUSINESS STATIONERY GRAPHICS 2
Pages: 224(192 in color) ¥16,000
世界の業種別レターヘッド・コレクション、第2弾
The second volume in our popular "Business Stationery Graphics" series. This publication focuses on letterheads, envelopes and business cards, all classified by business. This collection will serve artists and business people well.

SENSUAL IMAGES
Pages: 208(98 in color) ¥4,800
世界の官能フォト傑作集
We selected the best sensual works of 100 photographers from all over the world. The result is 200 sensual images concentrated in this volume. Page after page of photos that will quicken your pulse and stimulate your fantasies!

BROCHURE & PAMPHLET COLLECTION 3
Pages: 224(176 in color) ¥16,000
好評！業種別カタログ・コレクション、第3弾
The third volume in "Brochure & Pamphlet" series. Sixteen types of businesses are represented through artwork that really sell. This book conveys a sense of what's happening now in the catalogue design scene. A must for all creators.

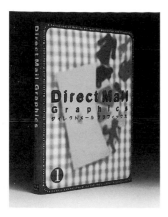

DIRECT MAIL GRAPHICS 1

Pages: 224(176 in color) ￥16,000
衣・食・住のセールスＤＭ特集！
The long-awaited design collection featuring direct mailers with outstanding sales impact and quality design. 350 of the best pieces, classified into 100 business categories. A veritable textbook of current direct marketing design.

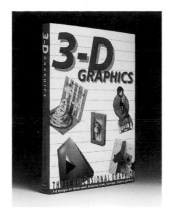

3-D GRAPHICS

Pages: 224(192 in color) ￥16,000
３-Ｄ・グラフィックスの大百科
300 works that demonstrate the best possibilities of 3-D graphic methods, including DMs, catalogues, posters, POPs and more. The volume is a virtual encyclopedia of 3-D graphics.

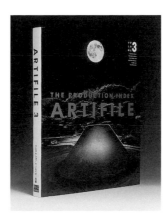

The Production Index ARTIFILE 3

Pages: 224(Full color) ￥13,500
活躍中！最新プロダクション年鑑、第３弾
Contributors are 116 top production companies and artists. See the artwork and read insightful messages from the creators.

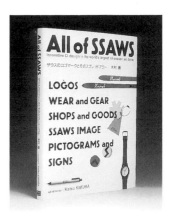

ALL OF SSAWS

Pages: 120(Full color) ￥8,800
サウスのＣＩ、アプリケーション ＆ グッズ
The graphics of SSAWS - the world's No.1 all-season ski dome is showcased in this publication; everything from CI and rental wear to notions and signs. This is the CI concept of the future - design that changes, evolves and propagates freely.

TYPO-DIRECTION IN JAPAN 5

Pages: 254(183 in color) ￥17,000
年鑑　日本のタイポディレクション'９３
314 award-winning typographic works from around the world are shown in this book. It includes recent masterpieces by eminent art directors and designers as well as powerful works by up-and-comoing designers.

T-SHIRT PRINT DESIGN & LOGOS

Pages: 224(192 in color) ￥16,000
世界のＴシャツ・プリントデザイン＆ロゴ
Volume 2 of our popular "T-shirt Graphics" series. In this publication, 800 designs for T-shirt graphics, including many trademarks and logotypes are showcased. The world's top fashion makers are featured.

POSTCARD GRAPHICS 4

Pages: 224(192 in color) ￥16,000
世界の業種別ポストカード・コレクション
Our popular Postcard Graphics series has been revamped for Postcard Graphics Vol.4. This new-look volume showcases approximately 1,000 varied examples selected from the world's best and ranging from direct mail to private greeting cards.

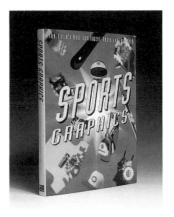

SPORTS GRAPHICS

Pages: 224(192 in color) ￥16,000
世界のスポーツ用品グラフィックス
An up-beat collection of 1,000 sporting-goods graphics from all around the world. This book features a variety of different goods, including uniforms, bags, shoes and equipment, and covers all sorts of sports: soccer, basketball, skiing, surfing and many, many more.

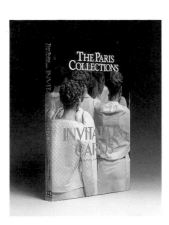

The Paris Collections / INVITATION CARDS

Pages: 200(192 in color) ￥16,000
パリ・コレクションの招待状グラフィックス
The Paris Collections are renowned for style and sophistication. Individual designers present their collections, and this volume features about 430 invitation cards for these shows, each mirroring the prestige and originality of the fashion house, and together encapsulating the glamour of Paris.

COMPANY BROCHURE COLLECTION

Pages: 224(192 in color) ￥16,000
業種別（会社・学校・施設）案内グラフィックス
Private companies, schools and leisure facilities - 220 informative brochures and guides, classified by type of business, from all sorts of enterprises and facilities throughout Japan. A fascinating and useful catalogue of imaginative layouts combined with effective design.

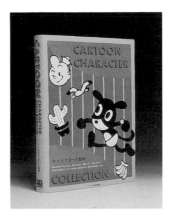

CARTOON CHARACTER COLLECTION

Pages: 480(B/W) ￥9,800
キャラクター大百科
A selection of 5,500 carefully chosen, quality cartoon drawings from the most successful illustrators in the business. Conveniently classified, the drawings cover everything from animals and natural scenery to food, sports and seasonal images. An encyclopedic collection and a useful source book.

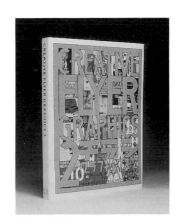

CREATIVE FLYER GRAPHICS 2

Pages: 224(208 in color) ￥16,000
世界のチラシ・グラフィックス２
This follow-up volume presents around 600 different flyers and leaflets promoting just about everything! From information on arts and music to advertising of food, consumer products and package tours, this selection demonstrates the power-packed design features of promotional flyers.